W9-BSI-890

FINDING A PASTOR

The Search Committee Handbook

Theodore A. McConnell

Winston Press

Cover design: Evans-Smith & Skubic, Inc.

Copyright © 1986 by Theodore A. McConnell.
All rights reserved. No part of this book may be reproduced,
stored in a retrieval system, or transmitted, in any form or by
any means, electronic, mechanical, photocopying, recording, or
otherwise, without the written permission of Winston Press, Inc.

Library of Congress Catalog Card Number: 85-51107

ISBN: 0-86683-493-1

Printed in the United States of America

5 4 3 2 1

Winston Press, Inc.
600 First Avenue North
Minneapolis, Minnesota 55403

Contents

Preface v

Chapter One: Choosing a Pastor 1
  An Enterprise in Need of Help 4
  A Process Gone Awry 6
  Some Common Pitfalls 10
    Too Large a Committee 11
    The Exhaustion Cycle 12
    The Early Autocrat 13
    The Far-Shores Syndrome 14
  Clergy Selection—Undertaking the Task 15
  Summary 15

Chapter Two: The Search Committee—Beginning the
    Task 17
  Committee Selection, Membership, and Size 17
  The Chair 19
  The Chair—Moving the Process 22
  The Committee's Role and Purpose 23
  Design for Operation 24
  The Parishioners and Their Needs 25
  The Regional Church Leadership 26
  The Outside Consultant 28
  The Interim Ministry 30
  Other Helps from Outside 31

Chapter Three: Gathering Names and Overcoming
    Some Roadblocks 33
  Compiling the List of Names 33
  Confronting the Exhaustion Cycle 35
  When the Chair Isn't Leading 36
  The Stalled Committee 38

72771

Commonly Shared Perceptions and Goals 38

Chapter Four: Visits and Interviews 41
The Committee Goes Visiting 43
The Committee Invites Candidates to Visit 45
Full Disclosure to the Candidates 48
Equal Consideration to the Candidates 50
Communications with Candidates 50

Chapter Five: Making the Final Decision 52
Moving from Visits and Interviews to the Decision 52
Reporting and Ratification 54
Informing the Candidates 54

Chapter Six: Negotiations 56
Conducting the Negotiations 59
What Should Be Covered? 62
Employment Contracts and Agreements 65
What More Is Needed? 76

Chapter Seven: It Doesn't End with the Call 77

Appendix: The Assistant Pastor 80
The Assistant Pastor's Post 80
The Search Process 83
When the Pastor Leaves 85

Further Reading 88

Preface

The purposes of this book are to provide a new perspective for churches and clergy involved in the calling process, to offer practical advice for improving the process, and to encourage a more intelligent and humane handling of the church's business when it calls a pastor. The book should also be of interest and use to seminarians preparing for ministry in those churches that use some form of committee to select and call clergy. In most instances, seminarians will encounter this process before graduation, and in the case of those serving internships they will meet it even earlier in their careers. The appendix chapter about assistant pastors will be of particular use, inasmuch as an increasing number of graduating seminarians begin their careers as assistant clergy.

A word should be said about the episodes or stories with which some of the chapters begin. Although the names of individuals and churches are fictitious, and some of the stories are composites based upon several experiences, each one is part of an actual event. The pointed stress and failure that these stories sometimes convey is not intended to discourage you but to serve as the basis for achieving a better result in your committee. Perhaps the matter will be remembered more easily because of these episodes, and the negative and positive experiences of others will be useful examples to guide you along a better way.

Particular appreciation and credit is due to my seminary classmate and longtime friend, Dr. Andrew Sorensen, now Dean of the School of Health Sciences, University of Massachusetts. His counsel and advice in reading much of this material has been of substantial assistance, and I acknowledge here his unfailing generosity of time and understanding. Similarly, the counsel and support of my best friend and wife, Molly Cochran McConnell, who is an expert and experienced editor, are immense. As in all other matters, her judgment and insight deserve my continued appreciation beyond expression.

This book is dedicated to the memory of my grandfather, Charles Merle Hornbaker, whose formative influence upon my life has been formidable and immense. It was from him, a firm-handed chairman of three different search committees, that I learned first about the clergy search and calling process.

Theodore Alan McConnell

Chapter One

Choosing a Pastor

Grover Rutledge is a decent and thoughtful minister who has tended the flock of Good Shepherd Church in the small town (2500) of Ridgecrest for twelve years. By all accounts he is a diligent pastor—somewhat unimaginative but careful, thorough, and considerate. He has counseled people faithfully, taught them consistently, and remained committed to his calling and the teachings of his church. Following college, seminary, and ordination, Grover took the advice of his church's officials and accepted a first position as an assistant pastor in a large urban parish. As with many "apprenticeships" there was considerably more undesirable toil than anything else under the senior pastor's assignments, and much of the learning was of a negative sort. There was usually more blame than appreciation from the senior minister, more youth work than a rounded diet of ministry, and little opportunity to officiate at worship or to preach. Nevertheless, Grover was committed and sufficiently patient and mature to endure this experience, believing that it was a first step along the way to becoming a pastor of "his own" parish.

Such arrangements, under less than sensitive or generous "commanders," lead to inevitable frustrations and despair. They are also blind alleys for most people. So after three years Grover and the senior pastor agreed that it was time for Grover to "move along." Living under the stress of this arrangement, Grover took the first offer that came along—from Good Shepherd, a small parish in a remote community. Now, twelve years later, Grover knows he is exhausted and burned out, and that a change of pace and place would be good for everyone—for Good Shepherd Church, its pastor, and his family. So Grover has gotten his availability file active with his church's national office, has contacted the regional placement officer, and for the past eight months has been submitting resumes to available parishes that have been listed as open. So far he has gathered a stack of form letter rejections from calling committees and one interview, in which it became clear that the parish was not willing to meet his present meager salary. Grover is perplexed and at times despairs of ever moving from Ridgecrest. Without badgering people or making a nuisance of himself, Grover has been active in following up leads and pursuing situations and placement officers. Everyone has assured him that his file looks good, that his recommendations are superior, and that they will commend him to open situations. How does he get past the form sifting stage of committees? How are calling committees really making their decisions?

* * *

Old First Church was led for thirty-five years by "dear" Dr. Weeks, whose retirement was celebrated with three gala banquets and a send-off retirement trip around the world. As a young man Dr. Weeks was in his second year at Old First as assistant to the octogenarian Dr. Green, when Dr. Green's sudden death resulted in Weeks' rapid promotion. With Weeks' impending retirement, an elaborate calling committee of twenty people was established. The committee was organized with numerous subcommittees, including a parish survey group, a resume evaluation group, scouting teams, and an initial interview group. To his credit, Dr. Weeks was meticulous in not making efforts to influence the choice of his successor. He did press the committee to seek outside counsel from the denomination's regional leadership and placement officer.

Following months of meetings and discussions, Old First Church's calling committee agreed upon a qualification profile that—as he confided to a close clergy friend—even Dr. Weeks wouldn't fit. Additional months were spent in unannounced scouting trips by various teams to all parts of the country. Some team visits resulted in initial interviews, but month after month the candidates suffered the similar fate of being cancelled out or blocked by one or another subcommittee. After ten months, during which many of the national church's leading clergy were passed over, one newly aggressive and vocal team presented the candidacy of Willie Brentwood, pastor of a modest suburban parish in a far distant state. Willie's candidacy was rushed through the subcommittees and the full committee, and he was called as Old First's new senior minister. Now, eighteen months later, Old First is in a mess, if not a downright shambles. Brentwood has turned out to be an unbelievably jarring opposite of dear Dr. Weeks. Where Weeks was a master administrator and captivating preacher, Brentwood is totally disorganized and a bombastic, erratic preacher whose penchant for personal trivia makes his sermons sound like advertisements for himself. Most church programs and patterns have been upended, and a sizable number of parishioners have departed for neighboring Second Church or the new but growing Mt. Zion Church. Moreover, Willie Brentwood is so homesick for his former state and close-knit, suburban, family-style parish that his speech is incessantly punctuated with "as we did this in Westwood" references. More than one member of Old First's calling committee has asked, "What went wrong?"

* * *

By all accounts Linda Johnson is the most popular and successful assistant pastor ever to have served Grace Church, River's Edge. In this large and bustling parish her five years of ministry have been phenomenal, and Gordon Jones, the senior minister of Grace, says, "I earnestly would like to have Linda here as long as I'm here, but I fully understand and support her desire to be pastor of a parish on her own. I can recommend her with absolutely no reservations, and I'll weep for myself and Grace Church if she leaves."

During the past two months Linda has been under consideration by a parish in which she is interested. After intensive background checks and two telephone interviews with committee members, Linda was invited to Messiah Church for a three-day visit. Following what seemed to be a very positive visit and interviews, Linda heard nothing from the committee for three weeks. Then, in the next three weeks, the committee's chairman had several telephone conversations with Linda, and another committee member called to review a list of hypothetical issues. Now the committee has asked if Linda would be willing to come back for another visit while they continue to consider another candidate. Conversations with the church's regional placement officer have not given Linda much solid information or evaluation of what is taking place. The telephone conversations have given her rather mixed signals about the committee's evaluation; at best, they are not coming to a clear and positive decision about her candidacy. Everyone seems to be floundering and lurching along in a seesaw fashion. Is it really worthwhile or advisable for Linda to spend more time with this situation?

*   *   *

An Enterprise in Need of Help

These three composites of actual experiences are but samples of the kinds of experiences encountered when a church calls a pastor. Many other stories could be told; those related throughout this book illustrate and examine various dilemmas, problems, and possibilities in the clergy selection process. This is a book written for those churches that use a committee system for selecting and calling pastors. Among such churches are Presbyterian, Lutheran, United Church of Christ, Episcopal, Baptist, and Disciples of Christ. Whatever else their differences in polity—and of course they are considerable—in all of these churches the calling of a pastor is *largely* a matter of local autonomy. It involves a process in which the local church or parish appoints a committee of its members to select a new pastor. This contrasts with the practices of the Roman Catholic and United Methodist systems, in which bishops appoint clergy to specific parishes.

It is beyond disputing that there is widespread anxiety, frustration, and dissatisfaction with how the committee selection process functions in many churches. Any person who has served on such a committee, or has even known someone who has done so, is likely to be familiar with these problems and the frustrations they cause. And rare are those clergy who do not have a reasonably high degree of dissatisfaction about this process. For local churches the problems posed by calling a new pastor are unique ones that present special obstacles and hurdles. If, for example, a church has been reasonably fortunate in having a long and happy incumbent, then it has not faced the selection process frequently, and there are not likely to be many experienced hands. If, in contrast, a church has gone through numerous clergy, then it is well acquainted with the process. However, other obstacles and barriers accompany specific parish situations: the small parish that has become a stepping-stone—either up or down; the seriously fractured parish; the decaying parish; the transition parish; the short-tenure parish; and so forth. In any case, the dislocations and displacements created by change in a local church's leadership are likely to be a source of anxiety, often accompanied by confusion and indecision.

Finding and employing a new pastor raises special concerns and tensions for any church. Church members often have widely divergent opinions about the kind of person who should be called. Because everyone wants the decision to be the right one, an unusually high level of tension may develop. What if a wrong decision is made? Getting rid of a pastor is a difficult and embarrassing business. A fractured or splintered parish can result. Because these complicated emotions and fears are part of the selection process, calling a pastor is one of the most crucial and unusual experiences confronting any local church.

Various larger church bodies have intermediate structures and processes to aid and assist local churches in the selection and calling process. Sometimes these function in a beneficial way, and sometimes they impede the process; but they can never offer the complete solution, because the decision-making remains with the local church. That is where improvements usually are needed, and that is what this book is about.

For clergy, the selection process can actually be a life-and-death matter, for it involves both vocation and livelihood. The stories of Grover Rutledge and Linda Johnson are not uncommon ones. Throughout this book I shall refer to other clergy experiences to illustrate the variety and intensity of problems posed by the committee selection process. Through bitter experiences, many clergy see themselves as unwitting and essentially helpless pawns in a procedure that is antithetical to what they believe, teach, and preach. All too often we have heard the comment "There ought to be a better way" when clergy are describing their experiences with the selection process. The extent of dissatisfaction with the process leads us to look at its liabilities in the hope that changes will eliminate the problems and generally improve the entire enterprise. I accept, for better or worse, the reality and permanence of the committee selection process as part of congregational autonomy, but I also believe that it can be improved greatly.

A Process Gone Awry

The stories of Grover Rutledge, Old First Church, and Linda Johnson are examples of a process that too often has gone awry in our churches. Their stories are not unusual or isolated. Conversations with clergy and lay people who have served on search committees throughout the country indicate that there is extensive dissatisfaction with clergy placement in churches, and that many people involved with it would like to see improvements.

The Reverend Paul Westman is an Episcopal priest and head of Educational Resources, Inc., of Narberth, Pennsylvania, a firm that provides educational and consulting services to numerous Lutheran, Episcopal, and United Church of Christ parishes. He is in a unique position to provide a national perspective of the clergy selection process. In a personal communication to me, Westman said: "Too often, despite good intentions and elaborate processes, the filling of a vacancy is best described as 'buying a pig in a poke'; conversely, many clergy find themselves running after the greased pig—one whose profile and potentiality is much less attractive to the winner once the race is won."

Westman's comment identifies several unnecessary and outrageous factors in the calling process today: procedures that are so elaborate and cumbersome as to block the very results for which they were developed; churches that are tied up for months with the process; churches that take a blind risk in calling a pastor; clergy that are misled and deceived (sometimes deliberately) by the process and information provided about parishes; clergy who are stalled or placed on hold for lengthy periods of time.

Browne Barr has been a noted and perceptive observer of the ministry for many years. As former pastor of Second Congregational Church in Waterbury, Connecticut, and then of First Congregational Church in Berkeley, California, and most recently as Dean of San Francisco Theological Seminary, a United Presbyterian Church seminary, Barr has a widely based perspective of the problems of churches calling pastors:

> I have been impressed by some aspects of the Presbyterian system which corrects many of the inequities of the less structured way the United Church of Christ goes about it. My biggest questions about the Presbyterian system are two: one, it takes so long that the church inevitably is tied up for months and months in the process; two, they require a self-study by the parish prior to the search. I feel that better management would postpone such intensive study until after a reasonably suited person has been called. Then the new minister and the parish

would move together into such a study, both would have ownership, and the gifts of the minister could be more effectively employed.[1]

Barr emphasizes the cumbersome and lengthy nature of the search process as it is now constituted in many places and rightly suggests that it could and should be changed. But his most startling suggestion is that churches have fallen into the proverbial trap of putting the cart before the horse as they engage in self-studies prior to the search and call. In this book, however, I follow that traditional sequence because it is the one that most churches follow, in one form or another, and because I want to see substantial improvements made in that process. Nevertheless, Barr's innovative suggestion should not be dismissed lightly, since the prevalent process may be the wrong one. For that reason alone the necessity for clergy leadership and training in dealing with aspects of the search and calling process is explored throughout this book. Perhaps it is sounder management and makes better sense for churches to engage in intensive self-study once a new pastor has been called. Then, as Barr suggests, the new pastor and the parish would move together through the study, coming to a commonly owned perception of themselves under new leadership.

Two special problems in clergy placement deserve attention and consideration in every church: (1) the increasing prejudice against calling pastors who are older, because they may not move on until retirement; (2) the all-too-common prejudice against women pastors. Writing in *Monday Morning,* a United Presbyterian clergy magazine, the Reverend George Douma, a retired pastor, speaks pointedly about the first problem:

> I have moderated enough churches to know the gut feeling of those who serve on pastor nominating committees. The fear of securing an older pastor, which sometimes means a person who has reached 45, is often brought to the surface. The concept goes along these lines: If we get a person in his or her late 40's or 50's, we might have that person as our pastor until retirement.[2]

Heaven forbid! Sometimes church people need to be convicted of their prejudice, and then something needs to be done to eradicate it. We hope that any committee that harbors this prejudice will find the resources and courage to overcome it. Working at the problem from a new angle, Pastor Douma suggests one experiment to improve the situation: Create a pool of clergy and churches that would commit themselves to designated ministries of five or six years, thereby insuring change in a planned, orderly fashion.

The placement of women clergy is one of the most difficult and vexing of issues in American churches. Dr. Yoshio Fukuyama, former director of research for the United Church of Christ's Homeland Ministries Board and now Dean of Chicago Theological Seminary, has spoken about this problem with particular insight and forcefulness:

> Recently I read a very moving account written by Carter Heyward about her journey to become a priest of the Episcopal Church. For those of us who belong to denominations where the ordination of women is not a problem, Ms. Heyward's experience in our day may sound unbelievable. After all, the United Church of Christ has over 400 ordained women clergy, more than any other mainline denomination.
>
> Obviously all is not well, even for those of us who ordain women into the Christian ministry. The increasing numbers of women pursuing Master of Divinity degrees (as well as majors in religious studies as undergraduates) suggest that the 1980's will challenge our churches and seminaries to face more squarely the need to change the institutional structures of our profession to give women clergy full and equal access to employment at all levels of the church's life. The restraints placed on women clergy are well known. They have been assigned to marginal positions in town and country parishes, as pastors' assistants or religious education directors, or to non-parochial ministries on college campuses, social service and denominational agencies. We rarely, if ever, see women called to senior positions of our larger congregations, to say nothing of medium-sized churches. The resistance of the church, and particularly of local congregations, to grant women clergy full participation in the profession is formidable.

Then Dr. Fukuyama continues:

Consider the evidence from the 1979 Salary Report of the Pension Boards of the United Church of Christ. In that year, women ministers were paid an average salary of $10,724 or $4,755 *less* than the average of $15,479 received by men!

What is even more distressing about this report is that the relative salary paid to women has actually *deteriorated* since 1976. In that year the difference in average salary was $2,953. Between 1976 and 1979, there was an increase of 39 percent in the number of women reporting. Since 1976, the average salary of male ministers increased 21 percent compared to only 8.6 percent for women!

Such discrepancies in compensation paid women and men are a problem affecting most occupational groups in our society. The Church's commitment to equal opportunity can hardly be served if women clergy are called in part to ease the economic responsibilities of our congregations.[3]

Dr. Fukuyama recently concluded: "There is a lot of talk about the frustrations women have in being placed, and particularly as they seek their second and third placement. However, not much seems to be done about the problem."[4]

Although it cannot be expected that the clergy calling process can be improved nationally in a brief time, it *is* time to begin making improvements on a large scale. The groups for whom this book is written, the search committees and councils in local churches, *can* begin to improve the process as they conduct their business. In time, the effect of local change and improvements will result in a better situation nationwide. In fact, practical changes begun at the local level—rather than top-down, national church programs—usually prove to be the most effective means to improve and change the existing situation.

Some Common Pitfalls

The local church calling committee faces a number of pitfalls and obstacles as it goes about its business. Four of the most common ones are: (1) too large a committee; (2) the exhaustion cycle; (3) the early autocrat; (4) the far-shores syndrome.

There are other pitfalls, but these four are encountered consistently and are the source of so many problems and troublesome decisions that we shall look at them in more detail. Identifying and labeling these pitfalls is the first step in seeking changes and improvements. Additional steps will be described in subsequent chapters.

Too large a committee

Old First Church's story is a good example of a committee that was too big to function effectively. Even for a parish of Old First's size, prestige, and prosperity, a twenty-two member committee was a cumbersome millstone. So much time and energy was expended in the mechanics of organization and preparation that the group's energy was depleted by the time it began actively to visit and evaluate prospective clergy. Moreover, the various subcommittees and teams began to block one another's efforts, especially where two or more teams were working at similar tasks.

The temptation is often strong to create a large committee in order to insure *full* representation of every group and viewpoint in a parish. A tiny parish of eighty-five members recently appointed a calling committee of twelve people! Not only was this a pretentious act, but every task from finding a common day for meetings to reaching agreements on basic issues and tactics became needlessly cumbersome. Generally speaking, the larger the committee, the more time-consuming is going to be its operation. Few people have the skills and superior control of procedure that the late Sam Rayburn, longtime Speaker of the U.S. House of Representatives, exhibited in guiding and managing large, cumbersome committees that dealt with complex motives, emotions, and desires. And yet, complex motives, emotions, and desires are exactly what are involved in a church's calling committee. Most people elected to chair such committees are likely to be severely strained by the task of guiding ten, fifteen, or twenty people in this complicated job. A smaller group is easier to guide. Finally, let's also state clearly what many people may think is a heresy but which I believe is a pragmatic and realistic truth: Large numbers do not necessarily mean democratic representation. A big committee is no guarantee of equitable representation for the membership, and it rarely bears any relationship to the job to be accomplished. If the job is to clean and rake the parish grounds as quickly as possible, then a large group of workers is a marvelous asset, but for other jobs a large group of people is too often a distinct liability. We will return to this topic in the next chapter, but suffice it to say at this point that considering the ability and quality of representatives, rather than the number, is the key to avoiding this pitfall.

The exhaustion cycle

Another pitfall that figured prominently in Old First Church's experience—and is often encountered by other calling committees—is the exhaustion cycle that sets in and intensifies with the passage of time. Most committees and churches have an innate time line, which may or may not correspond to an announced target date for reaching a decision. The time line has more to do with the dynamics, stamina, and pressures that develop within and act upon the committee than with anything else. Once the committee goes beyond this often-unrecognized time, it enters a new phase that usually is an erratic downward spiral. Things begin to fall apart or drift or become deadlocked. Although the process can be put back on the track in some cases, in others it will slip off again or be concluded with an uneasy compromise. The real danger of the exhaustion cycle is that once it begins, it often leads to a bad decision. Thus, although each committee is different and its members need to detect their own time line, six or seven months is a common dividing point, and committees that go beyond that time are more likely than not to experience the exhaustion cycle. In Chapter Five we shall turn to some suggestions for avoiding the exhaustion cycle or breaking it.

The early autocrat

Autocrats on calling committees come in many forms and manifest numerous pathologies: the local church's "lay dictator," a committee chair, the most troublesome fixture of the parish, or the most prominent or wealthy parishioner. In any event, early autocrats are intent upon imposing their will upon the committee without compromise. Almost invariably they will make their move *early on* (thus, *early* autocrat) to control the calling process, often seeking to chair the committee. Sometimes the autocrat already will have a candidate in mind; in other cases, the selection will be prompted by a favored recommendation or the initial chemistry in meeting a particular candidate.

The dilemma posed for a committee by the early autocrat is one of the most intractable of all, and often it simply cannot be resolved—especially if the autocrat is the principal source of financial support for the parish or is unscrupulous in conducting business. In such cases, the church's governing council, board, or vestry usually is a mirror image of the autocrat so that there is little or no opportunity to overcome the obstacle. Autocrats turn search committees into rubber-stamp committees. Where this is agreeable with the church's membership, it poses no particular problem, but when that is not the case, it is one of the most difficult problems to solve. If a sufficient number of people is mobilized, an autocrat may be deposed, but when it comes to church fights, people often run away from the problem or refuse to become involved. In most cases, nothing less than an outside force (Death is the most effective one!) can accomplish anything, and most regional church officials are *very* reluctant to intervene, even if they have the authority to do so.

A case that involved an unusual turn of events in the autocratic experience dramatically illustrates its dangers. A particularly prominent autocrat had installed himself as head of a church's calling committee as well as of its governing board. Following a decision by his chosen candidate not to accept the post, the autocrat was confronted with an overwhelming vote in favor of a popular candidate who had once served the church as an assistant pastor. In response to this ironic display of independence by the majority, the autocratic head arranged for the church's regional official to block the elected candidate by a variety of intimidating actions and threats. In the face of such tactics and the prospect of a less than cooperative beginning, the hapless candidate declined the call, clearing the way for the autocrat to continue imposing his will upon the local church.

The far-shores syndrome

In many calling committees the far-shores syndrome exhibits an exceptionally strong emotional pull. Usually it begins with the desire to find someone markedly different from the previous pastor, but it is difficult to comprehend why that desire is translated into action by presuming that *different* means located far away. Nevertheless, committees seem to be tempted easily into seeking someone from afar and overlooking the potential in their surrounding area. Sometimes this impulse is governed by the lure of the "unknown savior." Many committees are searching for a messiah-savior, and they usually find it difficult to see good old Dr. Brown from a neighboring community in that light. However, it just may be that good old Dr. Brown has much to offer, and he also may bring along a ready knowledge of the conference, presbytery, synod, or diocesan structure and personnel. Grover Rutledge had many positive qualities to offer a number of churches in his area, but being stuck in tiny Ridgecrest, he was overlooked or prematurely rejected by committees.

It is myopic to seek only candidates from afar and fail to canvass thoroughly one's geographical region. One of the frequently observed and tragic consequences of transplanting someone from a distant area is the social and cultural shock experienced by both new pastor and church. Some clergy are more adaptable than others, and, of course, the same is true of churches. The point to be emphasized is that the geographical factor should not be passed over lightly. It is often far more difficult to adapt from California to Pennsylvania or from Vermont to Arkansas than it is from Pennsylvania to New York or from Arkansas to Missouri.

Clergy Selection: Undertaking the Task

Put simply, the search committee's task is to find a new pastor for the church. However, as many committees have discovered, knowing what the task is and doing it are not quite the same thing. Doing the task proves to be anything but simple. Therefore, I suggest that the committee follow a set procedure as it begins its task. Subsequent chapters will develop the ten steps of the following sample procedure:

1. Organize the committee (members, size, chair).
2. Produce a statement of role and purpose.
3. Develop a design for effective operation.
4. Define the parish and its leadership needs (parish profile).
5. Consult and involve regional church leadership (outside help).
6. Select a slate of candidates.
7. Visit/interview candidates.
8. Evaluate candidates.
9. Make the final decision.
      or
   Return to Step 5 and proceed again.
10. Negotiate contract.

Summary

In this chapter, we have considered the difficult nature of the task confronting any church that seeks a new pastor, and we have pinpointed some of the fundamental factors and forces that impinge upon the process.

We have also tried to describe the extent of dissatisfaction with the committee selection process in order to point out the need for change and improvements. We have noted four common pitfalls into which many committees fall. Finally, we have proposed a ten-step procedure for search committees to use in calling a pastor. The chapters that follow will trace each step of that procedure and will offer suggestions for improving the selection process.

Footnotes

1. Browne Barr, in a personal communication of 24 March 1983.
2. George Douma, in *Monday Morning*, March 7, 1983, p. 15 ff.
3. Dr. Yoshio Fukuyama, "Leadership of the Church with Emerging Groups," *Chicago Theological Seminary Register*, Spring 1980, p. 1 ff.
4. Dr. Yoshio Fukuyama, in a personal communication of 14 March 1983.

Chapter Two

The Search Committee—
Beginning the Task

Organizing—selecting and forming—the search committee (Step 1) is the most important step in beginning the search process. For better or worse, the subsequent direction, duration, and conditions of the search will be determined by the kind of committee selected and its initial organization.

Committee Selection, Membership, and Size

Although there is considerable variety in how local churches select search committees, in most cases the council or governing board is involved in the process. In some cases, the council appoints the search committee; in others, the council nominates a slate that is submitted to a meeting of the church membership for election. Whatever the mechanism of selection, the most important issues to be decided are *size* and *composition*. In these matters are found the keys to success and efficient operation.

We have already mentioned (in Chapter One) that the size of the search committee is as crucial to its life and well-being. Generally speaking, churches tend to create committees that are too large and thereby immediately stumble into one of the most damaging pitfalls of the search process. Mere numbers do not insure a representative group or action. Indeed, in the case of a stacked or loaded committee, large numbers mean the opposite of reasonable and equitable representation. Moreover, the larger the committee, the more cumbersome are likely to be its deliberations, if for no other reason than the time involved in hearing everyone's viewpoint, settling conflicts, and building a consensus. Of course, such is not always the case—there are exceptions. With skilled and experienced leadership, even a large group can function better than some small groups. But there is no guarantee that skilled leadership will be available and selected in many churches, so emphasis needs to be placed upon the advantages of small committees and the drawbacks of ones that are too large. In general, small groups can move with greater speed and efficiency than large ones. Simply because fewer people are involved, the smaller committee's meeting schedule, group activity, and decision-making process are likely to move more smoothly and quickly than those of a large, cumbersome group. The model committee will be made up of five, six, or perhaps seven people. In most situations, five representative persons will constitute an effective committee.

To represent the church and its needs, the committee requires individuals who are seasoned, steady, and regular members. These are people who are capable of ascertaining the overall condition and needs of the church rather than just representing a special interest, quirk, or myopia. The *quality* of the committee's members will most likely determine the crucial issue of subsequent performance.

In addition to the qualities of vision, equity, and balanced judgment, a person's length and kind of church experience are of vital importance. In particular, search committees need members who understand and know well the beliefs, structure, and practices of their church. Those who are relatively new to a particular church or denomination are not the best candidates for search committees, because they have not yet gained the background and perspective of the church's tradition and practices. All too often, committees have reported disastrous experiences because one or more newer church members did not comprehend or support the beliefs, traditions, or practices of the church.

An understanding of the beliefs, structure, and practices of the church cannot be overemphasized in selecting search committee members. This is a prerequisite that should be waved only rarely. Whatever the advantages of an outsider's or newcomer's perspective may be, they are more than outweighed by the dangers of inexperience and lack of knowledge about a church's structure and practices. The search for a new pastor is neither the time nor place for an individual to attempt to remake a church, nor is the search committee the training and educational course for new members. Because the search process involves choosing a future for a particular church, those entrusted with that responsibility need the knowledge and experience of the institution in order to make their choice. Although this may seem to be so obvious that to mention it is to belabor the matter, it is simply astounding to discover how often search committees are dominated by, or confused and stalemated by, people who are new and inexperienced in the beliefs and practices of the church.

The Chair

When the pastor of Oak Hill Church announced his retirement, a ten-member search committee was appointed to be chaired by Sam Smith. Sam, a retired community figure, was a newcomer to Oak Hill Church, having been received into membership two years ago. There was considerable sentiment in the church's council for involving him in the church, and it generally was thought that he would have ample time to devote to the search committee. Although Sam appeared puzzled by the enterprise, he readily assented to the appointment and election. Throughout his life, Sam Smith had been an infrequent attender and never a participant in church life; he had become a member of Oak Hill Church only because of the persistent efforts of his wife, the retiring pastor, and friends in the church's Friday retirement club.

Sam took a lackluster approach to the job, calling only two meetings in six weeks following the committee's appointment. The first meeting was a rambling bull session in which no tasks, aims, or goals were clarified or decided upon. The second meeting was a more or less perfunctory session with the church's regional executive who told the group, "We're here to help if you tell us what you want!" Again, there was no organized agenda and little discussion of how to proceed or what steps would move the committee toward finding a new pastor.

Concurrent with the search committee's election, the Oak Hill Church council had decided to appoint an interim pastor for one year. Hugh Ellis, a sixty-nine-year-old retired pastor who had served two large, prestigious churches, was recommended to the council and appointed following an interview. Ellis' years of experience and energetic approach to the interim ministry led to an easy and quick acceptance of his leadership. And it wasn't long before some members of the search committee were seeking his informal counsel about the committee and in particular about Sam's nonexistent leadership. Not that this was any problem with Sam, for in the ensuing months he frequently said, "Well, let's have our pastor decide that; he's had experience in these things." However, other committee members also had experience in the process, and they were not so satisfied with this arrangement. In fact, several members had introduced the names of prospective clergy known to them and were eager to follow up with these names.

Hugh Ellis was able to be of considerable help to the committee in many respects, but he also had favorites among the clergy and especially among his many former assistants. In particular he was *very* eager to help Tom Winder, a former associate who was stuck in an assistantship in a nearby community. By most accounts Tom was a pretty lackluster guy who had spent his entire ministry as an assistant and therefore had limited experience compared to several other candidates. Moreover, he was only seven years away from retirement. Nevertheless, Sam Smith was easily persuaded by Hugh Ellis' careful but persistent suggestions, and a sufficient number of other committee members were similarly influenced by Dr. Hugh's hearty personality and heavy compaigning for Tom. The committee concluded its work after eleven months with a 6 to 4 vote for Tom Winder.

*   *   *

Sally Longacre was elected to chair the seven-member search committee of North Hills Church, and although she was exceedingly busy as a young physician, she agreed to devote the necessary time to the committee's work. In return Sally sought and readily obtained an agreement from the other committee members to make a similarly unrestricted donation of time and energy. Sally proved to be an excellent choice to chair the committee, for she was a clear, concise thinker and an orderly, results-oriented person who possessed considerable skill in dealing with people. Moreover, she was a *PK* (pastor's kid) who knew the church's structures and many of its clergy and had experienced the calling process three times in her own family. Sally moved swiftly to have the committee initiate and gather ideas about a new pastor from the various groups, committees, and boards of North Hills Church. From this informal process the committee produced a job description and candidate profile that was mailed to the membership prior to an open meeting in which the committee was able to receive additional information, comments, and criticism. This meeting gave the committee the data and impetus to produce a final description and profile quickly, making some adjustments and corrections from its original draft.

Working from this point, Sally led the committee as a whole in screening the resumes and recommendations of applicants supplied by the church's regional office. She also talked with a number of clergy and some seminary faculty whom she had come to know through her family's involvement with the church. As a consequence, Sally was able to obtain a number of valuable and candid appraisals of candidates and also add some new names to the North Hills list. After preliminary conversations with four candidates, the committee selected three to receive visits and formal interviews and then made a final choice. The entire process was completed in just over five months.

*   *   *

All that has been said concerning the makeup of the search committee can be repeated and added in double measure for the person selected to chair it. Depth and breadth of experience in the practices and traditions of the church, a comprehensive and sure grasp of the local parish, and skills of leadership in working with groups are called for in this demanding position.

Selection of the chair is the first item of business for the newly formed committee, provided a previous designation has not been made. In most instances this selection will be the first test or trial run of the committee, especially if it includes diverse and differing groups and viewpoints. As the members prepare to make this selection, they should attach particular importance to the chair's pivotal role. A weak or inept person in this post can mean a long, confusing, and difficult search. At the same time, an autocrat in the position can mean an equally difficult, strained, and frustrating experience. Somewhere between these extremes most committees include among their members that special person who is balanced and sensitive in thinking and acting, who has a clear grasp of the task ahead and can articulate it, and who is devoutly committed to Jesus Christ as Lord of the church. This is the person that you need to chair your search.

The Chair—Moving the Process

In following either the ten-step procedure described in the preceding chapter or any similar process, successful work depends on keeping things *moving*. Of course, orderly transactions of business, clear and open communications, and concise thinking are important factors, and we do not intend to skip lightly over any of them. But probably the greatest barrier to progress in getting the job done is in not keeping the search process moving. In most committees the chair is the key to whether the process keeps moving, proceeds in an erratic fashion, or bogs down. The chair needs to lead the group without running so far ahead as to lose them, and this often calls for considerable encouraging and coaching of the members.

Another key ingredient that the chair needs to establish at the beginning is the committee's wholehearted, shared commitment to the necessary time and work. Without this commitment, much time and energy is going to be expended in bringing absent members up-to-date and in coordinating schedules. A rather frequent obstacle is the too busy or absent member with whom serious misunderstandings arise because that person has not been involved in crucial deliberations. If, for whatever reason, members cannot give the necessary time and attention, they should be encouraged in a tactful but clear way to step aside for replacements who can make the necessary commitment.

The chair must also be capable of getting a consensus within the group, even on such mundane matters as meeting times and arrangements for visits and interviews. If a smooth pattern of consensus building can be established early in the committee's life, it usually will be easier to continue that pattern when deciding upon major issues. Once again, the skills of the chair, often supported by several other members, are the key to success. The work of Sally Longacre, whose broad range of experience in church life combined with her skilled ways with people and willingness to devote sufficient time to the enterprise, led to a model result. The process was kept moving at every step, and the sense of momentum worked in a positive and effective way. In contrast, the totally inexperienced, unskilled, and largely disinterested Sam Smith represented a disaster. Keeping the process moving without having it become a steamroller is fundamental to getting the task accomplished.

The Committee's Role and Purpose

Once the chair has been selected, the search committee's next order of business is to articulate clearly its role and purpose (Step 2), if this has not already been done by the church at large or by its governing body (see Step 6, Chapter Three).

Although the committee's obvious purpose is to find a new pastor, that is not its only purpose. To fulfill its task, the committee must discover its other purposes. The simplest way for the committee to begin that discovery process is to ask itself a few questions, such as the following:

- What theological and ecclesiastical norms and standards are given to the committee by the church?
- What other directions and procedures are provided or stated by the church constitutions, canons, governing rules, or traditions?
- Is an assessment or estimate of the state of the parish part of the committee's job?
- What guidelines and procedures are to be followed in conducting the search?
- What is the committee's relationship to the church's council and the membership at large?

These questions and their answers provide the basis for writing a clear and distinct statement of the committee's role and purpose. Producing a statement that is acceptable to the entire committee is an important and necessary exercise in working together, as well as in coming to a common understanding of the search.

Design for Operation

Once it has been organized, has selected a chair, and has written the general purpose statement, the committee needs to determine how it intends to operate as a group (Step 3). Among the questions it should address are the following:

- Will it work on each task as a committee of the whole?
- Will it have subcommittees or working teams/groups?
- Will individual members act for the committee on certain matters?
- If so, how much discretion and authority should be given to these members?

In order to work together, it is vital for the committee to develop a blueprint or design for operation so that all its members can agree on how they will proceed and on where they are going. This design should include a calendar of regular meetings, a division of labor among the members, and a timetable. Establishing a timetable for the committee's work as a whole, as well as for the work of each of its parts, is essential if momentum and progress are to be achieved and *the exhaustion cycle* avoided.

The Parishioners and Their Needs

The processes of developing a design for action (Step 3) and of defining the parish and its leadership needs (Step 4)—developing a parish profile—will take more time for some committees than for others, depending upon the group, the church's history, and its previous ministry. It is important to put together a clear parish profile with information about the parishioners and their needs. In some cases this profile may require a very informal survey, while in others it may involve the use of questionnaires and interviews. In any event, the search committee's aim at this juncture is to develop an accurate portrait of the congregation as quickly as possible. Once that is developed, the committee will need to check the validity of its findings. The profile must reflect accurately the congregation and where it is going or wants to go. Some committees have found it useful to distribute their draft profile to the congregation and then call for an open meeting to discuss it. The suggestions and results of such a meeting may then be used to produce a final version of the profile. In other churches, a more informal process of checking and consultation with the membership and the leadership of the various boards, committees, and working groups is used to test the profile.

Reaching an agreement on the nature of the parish and what it should seek in a new pastor is accomplished with relative ease and speed in some churches, whereas in others it becomes a lengthy and fractious experience. If an agreement is not reached at this stage, then the same issues are likely to emerge later in the search process and become the source of countless troubles for the committee. Therefore, it is preferable to spend more time at this early stage to reach an acceptable agreement than to devise a hasty compromise that some members of the committee assent to only grudgingly. Of course, any agreement about the nature of the parish and the kind of new pastor the committee should seek will involve certain compromises between different perspectives and desires. Nevertheless, without an agreement that the entire committee can endorse as theirs, it is impractical and foolish to proceed. Only when an agreement is reached and the profile is written into final form can the committee go on to the next steps of the search process.

Finally, the search committee must keep in mind that without the concentrated and continuing presence and involvement of all members in each task or step of the search process, it is likely to discover that it keeps going back to matters previously covered. This liability also points to the desirability of having a small committee, where it is less complicated to bring people together frequently and usually requires less time to reach decisions.

The Regional Church Leadership

Before seeking candidates, the search committee must complete its preliminary tasks and consult regional church leadership (Step 5). Various churches have quite different structural procedures for their regional leadership—synods, conferences, dioceses, state conventions, and presbytery executives, conferences ministers, presidents, or bishops. In some cases, regional leadership may require the local church to follow a fairly detailed and prescribed procedure in calling a new pastor, while in others the process is more informal and laissez-faire. In any event, the search committee should quickly establish ties to the regional leadership and then maintain a liaison throughout the search process. Some regional leaders take an active hand in the process, some delegate it to a personnel or placement officer, and others practice, in the words of Senator Daniel Patrick Moynihan, "benign neglect."

Few things a regional executive does are more important and potentially enduring than taking a personal role in clergy placement, yet many chief executives—be they bishops, presidents, or synodical leaders—delegate this job. The rationale usually given for this move is that the chief is too busy or that others can bring more specialized skills to the job. Although this may be so, it also is often the case that such chiefs are busy being busy—that is, not very well organized or efficient and terribly impressed with their role—or are seeking to remain aloof from the process so that no one will blame them for unhappy results. We think that clergy and churches deserve far better, more personal treatment and attention than this kind of approach, and we don't think that any committee should let itself be passed off in this way. Bureaucracies and bureaucrats respond to pressure sooner or later, although sometimes it has to be applied with persistence and increasing force in order to obtain results.

It is important for the committee to recognize that most likely they will have to take the initiative to obtain guidance and assistance. If a local church requires and wants substantial assistance, probably there will have to be considerable follow-up and bugging of the regional office and its executive. Of course there are churches that have been burned by aggressive regional leaders who have dumped a problem pastor on them. Thus, committees should be sufficiently wise and use common sense to evaluate the advice they are receiving and speak up loudly when they think that the advice is misleading or bad. Remember, for most intents and purposes, the local church is in the driver's seat. At the same time, it is important to appreciate the potential benefits that can be gained from forging a close working relationship with regional leaders: They are likely to have a pool of pastors and appraisals of them—often based upon personal observation; they are in a position to do some preliminary screening for the committee, thereby saving it time and preventing considerable wasted energy; they should be in a position to offer the committee a larger perspective of what is *possible* and *realistic*, given the available clergy and the particular church. This last item is a vital ingredient for success in accomplishing the committee's job.

We have already seen that realism in assessing a parish's strengths and limitations (Step 4, parish profile) is a necessary and vital step in conducting a successful search, but it is often missed. One of the most common failings of churches is to think more highly of themselves than they ought; this often results in chasing unrealistic goals and passing over able candidates. The sooner the search committee comes to a realistic assessment of what its church has to offer and what its needs are, the better. Sound regional church leadership can greatly aid committees in developing a parish profile that is usually more clear and realistic than if the committee tries to do it alone.

Generally speaking, we advocate more involvement by regional leaders in the search process, particularly in the initial stages. For example, we recommend at least two meetings of the committee and the regional executive at the beginning— an initial meeting in which both can gather impressions and information and then a second meeting within ten days or so, at which each has had time to reflect upon the first meeting and move to a new stage that is developed upon the basis of the first meeting. This provides everyone with something more than a perfunctory session; it keeps the process moving forward; and it just might result in forging closer and more meaningful long-term ties all around.

The Outside Consultant

In addition to seeking the services of the regional leadership, a growing practice among churches is employing an outside consultant to work with the search committee. Generally speaking, the justification for this practice is to provide the committee with an independent advisor who brings to the job a variety of skills and experience in conducting the clergy search process. In many cases the outside consultant's role is focused upon assisting the committee to work smoothly and effectively as a group, to develop a portrait or profile of the church, and to assess the backgrounds and abilities of candidates.

Some church organizations now mandate the use of outside consultants and may designate the person to be used. Other churches suggest or recommend using a consultant without designating a particular person or firm. If the decision remains with the committee, then names of possible consultants usually can be obtained from the church's regional office, from seminary deans or knowledgeable faculty, and in some instances from state or local councils of churches. The experience of another local church is often the most useful recommendation.

For the committee that is considering the use of a consultant, we advise an interview by the full committee in which the potential consultant is invited to make a presentation that describes the services to be provided. The matter of fees and payments should be thoroughly discussed in an open manner with the entire group. A presentation of this nature provides the opportunity to determine if this is the committee's kind of person. Needless to say, unless there is a positive attitude about the relationship, it is best not to proceed. A unwanted consultant, or one with whom the committee cannot function, simply will be an impediment to getting the job accomplished. For many churches, however, the outside consultant has proven to be an asset in many respects: Here is a "buffer" amid the dynamics of the search and calling process, an outsider whose perspective is based upon wide experience with the job, a third perspective alongside those of the committee and the church's regional leadership, and a person who can devote more time and attention to the committee's job than either the regional executives or a "supply" pastor.

Above all else, it should be recognized that the consultant's job is not to make the decision for the committee but to aid and assist it in functioning well. No church's search committee needs a head hunter who is in the business of digging up employment for people who have paid a large fee. A good consultant can provide guidance in organization and procedures, assist the committee through disagreements, and help to understand what is happening as the committee progresses from step to step. In many cases an able person chairing the committee can provide this leadership alone; in other cases an outside advisor may be needed.

The Interim Ministry

One of the first questions confronting any church when its pastor leaves is, Who will fulfill the clergy functions until a new pastor arrives? The two basic solutions are those of the supply ministry and the interim ministry. The supply ministry usually is a more limited form, in which a minister "supplies" Sunday services, certain other special services, and occasional emergency pastoral care. In contrast, an interim ministry assumes the full range of clerical functions and is usually contracted for a specific period of time—often six months to a year—or until a new minister arrives. One of the most common forms of interim ministry is that provided by a retired pastor. Indeed, in recent years a growing number of retired clergy have developed new careers going from one interim charge to another. Seminary faculty and other ordained persons with second careers are also sources for supply and interim ministries.

The role and function of the interim pastor vis-à-vis the search committee is a complicated and sensitive one, as is illustrated by the case of Hugh Ellis and Oak Hill Church. It can lead to difficult situations with disastrous consequences. Alternatively, it can provide much needed guidance and counsel from an experienced and seasoned pastor. Obviously, the relationship should be clarified thoroughly before the interim begins. The situation of otherwise unemployed clergy who perform interim ministries can become even more complicated if they become candidates for the vacant post. Of course, there are instances in which churches have found the best person in this way, having had the opportunity of a trial period. Nevertheless, unusual pressures are inherent in this arrangement, including those of campaigning for the post and ending the relationship if the committee is not in favor of the interim pastor. It is important to check church regulations and procedures if the committee begins to consider the interim pastor for a permanent position. In some churches it is stipulated in the organizational by-laws or constitution that the interim pastor cannot be a candidate for the post.

The role of the interim—or supply—as an advisor is a more complex matter. If that is to be one of his or her duties, then the details of that role should be specified in the interim's contract, much the same as they would be in contracting with an outside consultant. The most sensitive or complicated part of the status of the interim who advises the committee either formally or informally is due to the interim's special role and function as pastor of the church. The interim pastor is on location and so involved in the affairs of the parish (in contrast to an outside consultant) that unusual influence and weight easily become attached to the advice. And in cases like Hugh Ellis', it may result in the exertion of considerable pressure to make a particular selection. Generally speaking, that is an unhealthy situation and should be prevented.

The positive dimensions of the interim ministry—and they are numerous—include the provision of experienced counsel and guidance on a sustained basis. Moreover, interim pastors are in a unique position to assist the committee in keeping the process moving, for they are in daily contact with the church's life and needs and have time to devote to the task.

Other Helps from Outside

In addition to regional leadership, outside consultants, and interim or supply clergy, the committee may seek additional assistance from several sources. Foremost among these are the deans and faculty of seminaries related to a particular church. Usually these people will have considerable current knowledge about their graduates and often they are in a position to make recommendations and offer names that might not have come to a committee by the usual channels of communication. A committee should correspond with several seminaries, giving ample information about themselves and what they are seeking in a minister, and asking for names and recommendations. These inquiries should be followed up with telephone conversations or visits, if possible, to the schools. Names and addresses of deans and other appropriate seminary personnel usually can be secured from the church's regional office or from neighboring ministers of the same church. In many cases local churches have established relationships with a particular seminary based upon support or active involvement of previous clergy, and these should be the first place of contact.

Other potential sources of assistance and information are clergy and laity in nearby churches and, in particular, people who have served on other search committees. Often such people can provide considerable information and guidance that might not be obtained elsewhere. Their perspective is likely to give a committee another viewpoint. In fact, the entire search process could be substantially improved if presbyteries, dioceses, and state conferences developed pools or banks of experienced and capable people who could be made available upon a volunteer basis to local churches.

Chapter Three

Gathering Names
and Overcoming Some Roadblocks

In this chapter, suggestions are made to guide the committee in compiling its initial list of prospective candidates. Then some common roadblocks to the committee's progress are identified and discussed.

Compiling the List of Names

How does the committee compile a list of candidates' names? This question does not need to become a forbidding obstacle for any committee, although it happens in many situations. There is a variety of sources for obtaining names and recommendations, but in most instances the initiative for compiling a satisfactory list rests with the committee. The committee needs to recognize that this is the situation and take the initiative in the various directions suggested that follow.

In some churches a specified procedure must be followed in obtaining the names of possible candidates, whereas in other denominations the local church operates more or less on its own initiative and leadership. Whatever the case, the first calls and consultations are best made with the church's state or regional executive and clergy personnel or placement officer. Some regional executives operate by giving committees a suggested or recommended list of names and prefer that only those be considered. Other executives permit more individual initiative and flexibility in compiling the list. In either case, the committee needs to make a preliminary assessment of this list, based upon the information supplied about the names. This is an assessment to determine whether the committee agrees that it has a sufficient list or is dissatisfied and wants to seek additional names. Generally speaking, dissatisfaction at this stage comes when only two or three names are on the list or when immediate objections are raised to some names.

In order to assure that the field of possible names has been adequately surveyed or to enlarge the list, the committee can contact a number of sources including the following:
• Seminary deans and presidents
• Seminary placement and alumni offices
• College and university placement and alumni offices
• Other clergy in the denomination
• Councils of churches
• Denominational offices in other states and regions
• Editors of denominations' newspapers and presses
• Independent consultants
• Classified ads in denominational publications
• Classified ads in other Christian publications (e.g., *Christianity Today, Christian Century, Eternity*).

A letter of inquiry is usually the most desirable approach to these sources. This letter should describe the local church, what the church is seeking, and what it offers, and conclude by asking for names and recommendations. These letters should be followed up in approximately two weeks with telephone calls. These calls will develop a more personal contact between the committee and the sources and in many cases produce a quicker and more detailed response to the requests.

Seminary deans and president are often overlooked as a source of names of prospective candidates. They are an excellent source by virtue of their continuing contact with alumni and local churches. Similarly, church officers at both regional and national levels are in a particularly useful position to suggest and evaluate names based upon extensive contact with local churches and clergy. Other clergy known to committee members are another independent and potentially valuable source for names and recommendations. For the committee seeking a much broader but unevaluated list, placing ads in various religious publications and newsletters is a direct approach to clergy.

In the course of the committee's deliberations some common roadblocks frequently arise and these must be overcome if the search process is to be completed. Of particular importance are the problems of exhaustion, the lack of effective leadership, the stalemate, and the absence of commonly shared perceptions and goals.

Confronting the Exhaustion Cycle

In Chapter One the exhaustion cycle was described as one of the pitfalls into which search committees often fall. It is one of the most debilitating experiences and serious barriers to getting the job accomplished. Insofar as possible, a committee needs to estimate how much time it should allow for the search before it reaches the point of exhaustion. Then it should plan to accomplish its job before reaching that point. Making this determination is never easy, because it involves the complex interactions of a group, but under skilled leadership such a calendar can be established. To be certain, the calendar may need to be revised due to later developments. But again, this needs to be the result of a commonly agreed-upon change. Once the calendar has been established, it is vital to stick to it in order to avoid entering the exhaustion cycle. In some cases, this task will fall upon the chair, who must be astute in sensing changes within the group and signs of approaching exhaustion. When these signs are detected, they need to be discussed and faced by the committee as a way of beginning to reverse the slide into the downward spiral.

What is to be done when the cycle has set in? Can it be broken? Obviously that depends on the people involved and the committee's process. In some cases, the cycle can be broken most effectively and quickly with the assistance of a skilled outside counselor or advisor who can help the committee get a perspective on what has happened and can recommend some strong measures to break the pattern. These may include reorganizing the committee, taking a rest period and then beginning again, or even throwing out all of the dead-locked or undecided candidates' names and starting a new search.

Choices made in the exhaustion cycle are seldom good choices. There are too many examples of committees like that of Old First Church and Willie Brentwood (Chapter One), where selections made in the exhaustion cycle have proven to be colossal blunders. It is a common fallacy, born of the frustration and confusion of exhaustion, to think that the only way to end the matter is to settle on a compromise candidate or the first new name to appear. This is exactly what should *not* be done, for it joins together two incompatible matters. Resolving the exhaustion cycle *is* a prerequisite to selecting a candidate, but that selection should never be the product of exhaustion. Rather, the exhaustion cycle must first be broken; then, and only then, should a new, fresh phase begin, in which the committee can move toward a positive choice.

When the Chair Isn't Leading

The experience of Oak Hill Church and Sam Smith (Chapter Two) is not uncommon among search committees. Unfortunately, for many reasons weak persons who cannot lead or those lacking a church background and experience often get elected and appointed to chair search committees. And as we have seen, because so much of the committee's work and its success or failure is dependent upon the chair, it is a major problem when that person isn't leading. Given the nature of human personality and the complex dynamics of church life, weak chairs will seldom step aside, regardless of the difficulties or failure they may be creating.

What can a committee do when it becomes increasingly apparent that the chair isn't leading and probably isn't capable of doing so? Here is another situation where an outside consultant or a skilled interim or supply pastor may be the most effective answer. If such persons are already on the scene, then utilizing their help is the best path to follow in seeking a solution. Working *through* the chair and using extensive guidance and coaching, the consultant may establish leadership. Quite obviously, this procedure can be a tenuous one that requires a sufficiently amicable chair as well as an objective and even-handed advisor if it is to be successful. Other capable committee members are an additional asset in such a situation.

Without the presence of a consultant or interim pastor, this leadership burden falls to the rest of the committee or certain of its members. The ever-present danger in such situations is that a committee will become divided and polarized. This, in turn, can easily lead to the sad and bitter consequence of a split church. The first step in moving forward, once a committee is in substantial agreement about a weak chair, is to seek one or more consultations with the church's regional executive or placement officer. The rationale will be: "We need some consultation because we don't seem to be getting anywhere." In some churches the regional executive has authority to enter the local church and resolve such problems, while in others the situation is a more ambiguous one, resting upon the executive's powers of persuasion and skills to bring about a solution. In any event, this step will usually move matters toward a solution, granted sufficient perception and skill upon the part of the regional executive.

It may well be that in concert with the executive—or independently—a committee will come to the conclusion that it needs an outside consultant or advisor. This is a somewhat unusual step to take in midstream; but if it can be taken with reasonable agreement, then it should be done. Bringing an outside advisor into the leadership vacuum is more likely than anything else to resolve the problem, for it brings to the situation a new person who is neither part of the committee nor the chair, but who has special experience and skills invaluable to both.

The Stalled Committee

Sometimes search committees become stalled. If this happens, the first issue to be determined is whether it is a temporary matter or a permanent deadlock. Through one method or another, the committee must assess what has happened and attempt to reach an agreement on its perception of itself. The committee that is stalled only temporarily can usually get moving again by using one or more of the procedures that we have already discussed: involving the regional executive; bringing in an outside advisor or consultant; using the interim or supply minister as advisor; or seeking the aid of experienced veterans of the search process from other local churches.

When a committee becomes deadlocked, however, the situation is more serious. Sometimes the impasse can be resolved by using one or more of the procedures mentioned above, but often the matter is simply hopeless and should be so declared. In such a case, the radical step of dissolving the committee is the only realistic solution. A deadlocked committee should not continue in existence indefinitely, but should have the honesty and courage to resign and dissolve itself. Far too frequently, deadlocked committees grimly grind on, bickering and fighting and then finally making a decision that contains the seeds of disaster because one side has forced its will upon the other. Irreconcilable differences need to be faced squarely for what they represent, lest they persist and endure. The shock of dissolving a committee *should* lead to a full and open discussion of the issues by the entire church's membership, for it is only in this way that a new beginning is possible. St. Paul knew a great deal about these matters, and his two letters to the fractious churches at Cornith are the very best point for beginning anew. They should be read, studied, and thoroughly heeded by any church before it forms a second search committee.

Commonly Shared Perceptions and Goals

This chapter has been concerned with resolving problems and removing barriers to getting the committee's job accomplished. Now I would like to draw attention back to that part of the search committee's experience that most affects all of its work —the extent to which it reaches and sticks to common perceptions and goals of its job (see Step 2).

One of the reasons the North Hills Church committee chaired by Sally Longacre (Chapter Two) was able to function so effectively and smoothly was that Sally was able to help the group to agree on how it perceived the church's nature and needs and then to set its goals in light of those needs. The importance of beginning the committee's work with these common agreements may sound elementary and obvious. Yet the failure to accomplish this at the beginning is one of the most frequent sources of later problems and disagreements. Without a common perception of where the church has been and where it is going, it is highly unlikely that a group can come to an agreement on a new pastor. The failure at the outset to reach a consensus on perceptions and goals often manifests itself in disagreements over seemingly minor matters that have a way of developing into major barriers. It is always a sound investment of time and energy to reach this consensus before proceeding to other matters.

For some committees, reaching such a consensus may prove elusive, if not convulsive. This is often the case when the committee is a large and diverse one in which people hold little in common. Although such diversity may mirror the spectrum of people in a church, it is more than likely to lead to a total deadlock when it comes to decision making. And although I am not suggesting that every committee should be only a group of the like-minded, it is necessary to come to a fairly broad area of mutually shared perspectives in order to get the job accomplished.

One recent example is a small church (under 100 members) that included a highly heterogeneous mixture with such strongly held viewpoints all around that they had totally conflicting perspectives of the church's needs and goals. One group, for example, strongly believed that the church should become involved with a broad range of social concerns, including demonstrations against war and military armaments, support for welfare aid, income assistance for the poor and needy, and development of worldwide food programs. These members were personally involved in many of these causes and believed that it was important to be so identified as church members. Other members of the church were vocal in their opposition to such involvements and strongly advocated a church and ministry that would be strictly oriented to the pastoral care of its own members.

The twelve-member search committee reflected the full range of viewpoints along this spectrum and quite predictably became involved in a protracted tug-of-war over what kind of pastor to call. This committee wrote a profile and goals that listed all of the alternative viewpoints and attached equal weight to each. In effect, it avoided coming to a set of common perceptions and goals and proceeded directly to reviewing names and interviewing candidates. The failure to resolve these matters or reach some practical compromise about them manifested itself in disagreements that erupted throughout the review process and in interviews with candidates. The search for a pastor to satisfy all of these demands was unrealistic. In this case, the outcome was determined by an exercise of power on the part of the patron and principal contributor to the church, whose solidly safe, hand-picked candidate was forced upon the committee and the church, thereby insuring the continuation of intense bickering and several splits.

For other committees and churches—and they are the majority—there is a wide area of common understanding among the members about who they are and where they are going. In these cases it is a relatively routine process to identify and reach agreements on the church's nature, needs, and goals. When this is accomplished and put into written form, it serves as the basis for conducting the search for a new pastor. By making it the first task of the committee and not moving on until it is accomplished, the remainder of the committee's job will be made much more simple, clear-cut, and easy to accomplish.

Once the shared perceptions and goals have been agreed upon and a list of candidates has been evaluated and narrowed down to the promising names, then most committees are ready to begin visits and interviews.

Chapter Four

Visits and Interviews

When Washington Square Church, a large, center-city parish, began its search for a new pastor, the search committee adopted a three-step interview process that included: (1) unannounced visits by individual committee members to Sunday services conducted by prospective candidates; (2) announced return visits by small visitation teams of three or four members; (3) select invitations to candidates to visit Washington Square for formal interviews. The first and second steps of this process involved nearly a year of activity, covering visits to churches located from New York City to San Francisco. Throughout this extended time, the major emphasis of the search was placed upon the unannounced visits and the follow-up visits by the "flying teams." Many candidates were eliminated at the first step and several (but markedly fewer) at the second, leaving an invited list of eight for the final step and decision.

*　　*　　*

After extensive sifting of resumes and applications, the search committee of Messiah Church, a small parish of 100 members, made extensive use of telephone interviews and conversations. In addition to the practical necessities of an exceedingly limited budget, the committee was intent upon avoiding waste time and energies in finding a new pastor.

Those candidates selected by the committee for further consideration were contacted by telephone calls from the chair, who used these initial conversations to get a feel for the person, as well as to ask some specific questions raised by the committee in reviewing the candidate's resume and credentials. When the results of this step were positive and seemed to warrant further exploration, the committee proceeded to a second step, a conference call in which the entire committee met in the chair's house and, using a special telephone device, conducted group conversations by long distance. Careful advance planning of the format and outline of these calls led to productive use of the time and prevented diffuse and rambling conversations or pauses and silences. From this second step the committee was able to select two final candidates who were invited to visit the parish for two days of conversation and interviews.

*   *   *

Washington Square Church and Messiah Church are examples of two different approaches to handling visits and interviews of prospective pastors (Step 7). In one sense, they are used to illustrate the two extremes: one involving an elaborate, lengthy, and costly plan that emphasized first-person contacts; the other involving a minimal monetary investment made necessary by a barebones budget. Between these alternatives, a range of possibilities can be envisioned, depending upon the particular church and its needs, resources, and location. Whether the search committee begins this part of its search with visits to prospective candidates or by inviting candidates to come and visit the committee, it needs to concentrate carefully on the objectives of visits and interviews and to have some practical guidance for handling them.

The Committee Goes Visiting

To find the right candidate, some committees choose to send out scouting teams or individuals unannounced (as did Washington Square); others make appointments for an initial visit by several committee members; and still others go visiting as a committee of the whole. The purposes of such visits are to develop some personal acquaintance with candidates, to observe them in a local church setting, possibly to attend a worship service conducted by candidates and hear them preach, and to meet for a preliminary discussion of interests, needs, and expectations.

The unannounced (to the candidate) visit is the most controversial kind of visit, and the basic question to be asked about it is, "What do you expect to accomplish and why are you going about it in a covert and secretive way?" Generally speaking, the possible values of such visits are vastly overrated. Moreover, they establish a certain style and image that are questionable for any church. Probably nothing can be observed or gained in an unannounced visit that cannot be gained by reasonably astute and common-sense observation during an announced visit. Moreover, the announced visit establishes a clarity and openness at the beginning that can set a positive atmosphere for subsequent relationships.

Visits to candidates by only one member of the committee can also lead to a dangerous pitfall: an initial decision based solely upon one person's appraisal. On the one hand, this procedure may result in significant losses for the search, when candidates are eliminated on the basis of a solitary judgment. On the other hand, such visits may lead to an unfortunate promotion of one candidate prematurely. There is a clear and distinct advantage in having all visits made by several committee members. Not only is a fuller and more measured appraisal likely to be gained in this way, but candidates are insured of getting a more representative and complete picture of the calling church.

When planning visits, the committee should contact candidates well in advance by mail or telephone in order to arrange a productive and efficient schedule. The committee should be open and clear about its purposes and the present state of its search process. In the initial contact, something like this needs to be said: "We would like to come for a preliminary visit to get acquainted and begin to explore the possibilities of ministry. You are one of (number) candidates that we are visiting, and when these visits are completed, we expect to then select (number) candidates to invite for visits to us before making a final decision. Our present schedule calls for us to complete this first stage by (date)." This kind of specific and forthright introduction dispels any ambiguities and provides candidates with a clear picture of the process. Subsequent communications—even postcards—will keep candidates informed about the progress of the search. Such common courtesy and considerate action are always appropriate. It is both surprising and appalling how often committees fail to provide candidates clear, simple, and forthright information about what they are doing. Nevertheless, it can be done without compromising deliberations in any respect, and it eliminates confusion, needless suspense, and bad feelings.

When visiting candidates in their present churches, committees need to be especially attentive to the sensitive nature of the situation. They are present to consider prospects for calling persons away from their present ministry, and this is a venture that can generate considerable gossip, embarrassment, and even resentment if it becomes generally known in the candidate's parish. Quietness, reserve, and care need to be exercised when the committee includes a Sunday worship visitation; inconspicuous entrances, seating, and exits are in order.

An example of what *not* to do in such situations is this case. A six-member committee visited the 11:00 A.M. worship of a church located in a suburban residential area with little traffic. Having flown to the region, the committee did not have the common sense to rent a car but took a taxi, which made their arrival all the more conspicuous in that area. Six strangers departing from a taxi directly in front of the church building ten minutes before the service was a clear announcement, and within minutes various parish members were passing the word and speculating about the visitors. Needless to say, this was a disruptive and embarrassing visit. In this case, the committee happened not to call that particular pastor, but their clumsy visit became the source of difficulties that could have been prevented by following these two, simple guidelines:

• *Plan the committee's arrival to be as discreet and unobstrusive as possible.*

A block of strangers seated together in one pew is going to be an immediate object of attention in many churches. Thus, the committee should also:

• *Stagger its entrances and seating to give less attention to its presence.*

In initial visits it is quite acceptable to schedule a luncheon or dinner with a candidate. In fact, such plans are preferable to holding a conversation in the parish office where there is likely to be considerable traffic and awareness that something is going on.

The Committee Invites Candidates to Visit

Once the committee has decided upon a list of candidates it wants to invite to visit the parish and be interviewed, some additional group discussion and considerable advance planning is needed. Prior to any visits or interviews, the committee needs to articulate clearly what it is seeking to accomplish in the visits and interviews and how these goals are to be attained. That is to say, an unplanned, free-floating visit or interview is likely to be unsatisfactory to both candidate and committee. Instead, the committee should first develop in writing a list of questions and items for discussion. Part of this list should include questions to be asked of all the candidates; a second, smaller part should cover any specific items related to particular candidates, as suggested from prior contacts and conversations or consideration of applications and resumes.

During the actual interview, some committees may prefer to designate specific members to cover certain questions; others will arbitrarily break up the lists into parts; and still others will choose to have the chair introduce each item and cover the list. In some cases, committees may send candidates an advance list of topics and questions; others prefer to have unprepared sessions. There are advantages and disadvantages to both procedures, but in the balance we suggest that having candidates handle a variety of questions without having been able to prepare responses is more likely to provide insight into the candidates' general approach and outlook.

A schedule for the entire visit of each candidate should be carefully planned and written down in advance of the visit. The committee should describe the specific process and procedure it will follow so that the candidates know what will be taking place and where they are in the process. It is always a good idea for the chair to summarize these matters briefly at the opening of the meeting. This accomplishes two purposes: It again makes clear for everyone what has been said previously; and it pinpoints the meeting's aims and purpose. Although these may seem to be minor details that everyone assumes and knows, it is foolish and misleading to assume anything. People hear and perceive differently; people do not tell other people; people forget; etc.

An example of the failure to have clear and explicit planning and communication is the experience of a search committee that had chosen to work through a three person subcommittee for screening candidates. The subcommittee invited five candidates to visit the parish for first-round interviews, after which two or three candidates would be selected for a return visit with the entire committee. However, none of this procedure was explained to the candidates, who were left in an atmosphere of secrecy, guessing, and bewilderment. When initially invited, they were told neither that this was to be a first round with a subcommittee, nor when they might meet with the full committee, nor where they stood in the process, nor what schedule was being followed.

Therefore, when inviting candidates to visit, keep the following guideline in mind: *Be thoroughly explicit and clear about the process and the schedule that you will use.* You can do so without compromising any of the committee's decisions or deliberations.

In planning schedules for visits, whether of one day or more, allow ample time for the formal committee interview as well as for a leisurely tour of the parish's physical facilities and a brief tour of the town or city. Providing candidates with a packet of informative printed materials about the community is also very useful and appreciated. This packet may include literature available from the local chamber of commerce, the municipality, the county, various service organizations, public institutions, and industries. Include information about schools, the parish neighborhood, and a good map of the local area.

In almost all situations, the committee will not be making its final decision after this first visit. In many cases there will be other candidates' visits, followed by a decision to call for a second or return visit with one or two candidates. Whatever procedure the committee decides to follow, it should be clearly and openly described to each candidate.

During the actual visit, either the chair or another designated person should act as the host and guide for the candidate. It is important that the host be a balanced and reasonably objective representative of the church and community so that the candidate is given a full perspective of the situation, and is not subjected to some special interest or an unduly biased opinion. Every region and every parish has its pluses and minuses. Although the committee should strive to put its best foot forward, it must do so in a reasonable and realistic way. Honesty combined with true hospitality will do more to sell the candidate than the slickest sales pitch.

During visits the committee may wish to introduce candidates to other members of the church who are not part of the search committee. These people may have had a long involvement with the church, or prominent leadership in the community, or other leadership in the church. Such introductions and conversations are best arranged on an informal basis in homes or for meals. If there is extra time available, it may be useful for candidates to meet the pastor of a neighboring parish, especially one of the same church or tradition. Of course, this depends upon the local situation, but this kind of opportunity can provide candidates with a potentially important outside perspective about the community.

During the formal interview, the chair should introduce the session with a summary of the candidate's resume, a recapitulation of the search process and what is about to take place, and an outline of the interview's structure. While the interview is going on, the chair should seek to keep the conversation moving without closing off discussion too quickly. It is also important to draw out the concerns and responses both of the entire committee and of the candidate. At the end of the session the candidate should be given an opportunity to ask questions of the committee and to address any additional matters.

Each committee will have its particular list of concerns and questions. The committee should also describe to the candidates clearly and explicitly that list, the parish, and the parish's pastoral needs. If these are not clearly perceived and articulated, then you are not ready to conduct interviews and visits.

The chair or the candidate's host—or both—should give special attention to seeing that good etiquette and common courtesies are observed throughout each visit. These include punctuality, complete planning for room and board and transportation, and allowing adequate time for each event and conversation. Finally, all the candidate's expenses should be handled in a forthright fashion and prompt reimbursement made. When you invite a candidate to make a visit, all travel and related expenses are your responsibility, and you should take the initiative to get an itemized list and to process it for payment.

Finally, committees should recognize that visits and interviews are two-sided events: You are looking over candidates, and candidates are also looking at you. The way in which you handle the entire visit, including the little details, forms a very important part of your church's image and reputation.

Full Disclosure to the Candidates

Although this may seem to be an odd or even an inappropriate topic, experience indicates otherwise. One objective or goal of every search committee should be to provide candidates with a full and complete story about the parish, including its past and present, its losses and gains, and its strengths and weaknesses. In particular, a full disclosure regarding the church's finances should be given.

A brief but adequate description and review of the past ministry of the church should be provided in a matter-of-fact manner. This is an area where there are usually widely different perceptions and opinions strongly held by different people. It is probably best for this subject to be discussed during the formal interview so that the entire committee can comment. If there are disagreements regarding perspectives and appraisals of the past, they should be clearly indicated in a straightforward manner. It then becomes a matter of the candidate's judgment to determine if further discussion or follow-up is needed. The committee's objective is simply to make an honest, full, and clear disclosure without becoming involved in reliving the past.

Conversations in recent years with numerous clergy and laity lead me to take special note of the statistics and data that search committees give to candidates, particularly those concerning membership and parish finances. One hears of too many instances (One would be too many!) where churches and their lay leaders have given false or misleading data to candidates, usually in order to conceal a bad problem or difficulty. This deception may be undertaken by a well-intentioned lay leader—sometimes by way of embarassment, sometimes out of frustration and desperation in not being able to secure a pastor, sometimes as a simple and brazen deception to make things look better. In any event, the motivation is not the important matter. The matter of importance is that the *only* procedure for any search committee is to provide honest, complete and clear statistics about the parish. The practice of fraud or deception and the use of misleading or incomplete data have absolutely no justification or defense in any hiring enterprise, but especially in the church.

Equal Consideration to the Candidates

A concluding word should be said concerning the consideration given to candidates throughout the search and selection process and especially during the usually exhausting, time-consuming, and expensive stage of visits and interviews. The search committee should make it an absolute rule that *equal and fair consideration be given to all of the candidates interviewed.* If you cannot give candidates *equal* consideration, do not invite them for a visit or interview.

Communications with Candidates

As churches have increasing numbers of candidates and applicants for vacancies, the matter of keeping them informed during the search process takes on greater importance. One of the most frequently heard complaints from clergy is that search committees handle communications poorly and fail to keep them informed. We believe that it is possible to follow some common standards of etiquette and courtesy and that not to do so is inexcusable. Clergy inquiries and applications deserve a *prompt* reply or acknowledgment—even if it is just a form letter—and *not* two or three weeks after they have been received.

As soon as a decision is made to pass over a candidate's name, the person should be informed and not kept in suspense. There is no good reason for waiting until the process is completed before notifying people that they are no longer under consideration. During the search process there may be some periods during which no decisions are taking place, and in cases of stalled committees this can continue for a lengthy period of time. If four weeks elapse in communications, I recommend sending a simple form letter that states that the person's candidacy continues under active consideration but that more time is being required by the committee. This is a small but significant gesture in public relations, as well as common courtesy.

What is said and how it is said are of substantial importance in the committee's communications, and particularly in telling people that their names have been eliminated or passed over for another candidate. It is not easy to write a diplomatic and kind rejection letter, yet there is needless harm and damage done by a crudely phrased or brusque one. A brief letter stating the decision and then expressing some best wishes for the person's future is sufficient. One need not be effusive in these communications, but a coldly worded "This is to inform you" letter is both tactless and shows a lack of human consideration upon the part of the writer. One of the nicest rejection letters that we have seen in recent years was sent by the chairman of a search committee that had received over one hundred names and applications. At the bottom of a factual and courteous letter, he had penned a simple sentence: "It was awfully hard making this decision because there were so many fine candidates, including you." That small note was a gesture that made it easier for people to take the bad news of the letter and to end the matter with an impression that they had been dealt with in a humane way.

Such details and additional communications, as we have mentioned above, require time and effort. Committees should make that effort, for the business of the church needs to be conducted according to the highest standards and with keen attention to humaneness and dignity. The example set by the committee in how it conducts its business and relates to people is of the greatest importance for the entire church and its ministry.

Chapter Five

Making the Final Decision

Moving from Visits and Interviews to the Decision

Evaluating candidates (Step 8) and making the final decision (Step 9) often follow each other quite smoothly and rapidly for committees. In such cases the committee's next step is relatively simple: Hold a formal committee session in which the decision is made by vote, using whatever rules have been selected or specified by the particular church (for example, a simple majority vote or a two-thirds plurality vote). Once the final selection has been made, you should make a recommendation either to the church council or directly to the church membership, depending upon the structure and governing rules of the particular church. (For convenience, we shall use "council" for the governing body of the local church, variously called the council, the session, the consistory, the vestry, the board of trustees.) In some cases, where the church council makes the final decision and selection, it may ask the committee to recommend more than one acceptable candidate.

In considering the search committee's work in making a decision or recommendation, some attention needs to be given to those instances where obstacles arise in finding a consensus and reaching agreement on a candidate. Once the interviews have been completed, the most common obstacles to a final decision are a committee divided between two candidates and a committee divided over one candidate. Reaching an agreement in these situations often proves to be difficult and time-consuming. The *exhaustion cycle* (see Chapter One) is more likely to set in at this point, too, leading to a poor choice that involves unresolved disputes. The role of the chair is crucial and decisive in such instances:

- Has the chair been sufficiently attentive and perceptive in hearing and understanding the various viewpoints within the committee?
- Has an adequate attempt been made to find an acceptable solution or compromise?
- Has an overall perspective been developed that could suggest the right solution?

Without attention to these matters, resolving the dilemma is going to be especially difficult.

In some situations, this is precisely the point at which calling in an outside advisor or consultant could be useful. Breaking any kind of deadlock or stalemate may be accomplished more easily with the help of an outside advisor. On the other hand, if the chair has not become strongly involved in one side or the other, the chair may be able to bring about a conclusion. Generally speaking, patient attempts to do so should be tried before seeking an outside consultant.

It is important not to let a deadlock continue indefinitely. If it cannot be broken with a compromise vote within one or two weeks, the chair should move for dissolution of the search, a dismissal of all the candidates' names, and the initiation of an entirely new search (go back to Step 5). In some situations it may prove more practical and advisable to begin anew than to have a compromise that really is not accepted. In other words, a compromise that involves continuing ill will and bickering is not a compromise but a one-sided victory forced upon the other side. In such situations the compromise candidate enters the church facing an impossible task and future. Only an uninformed or truly desperate candidate would undertake such a burden. Under such circumstances it is preferable to begin a new search and try again with a new committee and new candidates.

Reporting and Ratification

Once the search committee has made a final selection, a procedure of reporting and ratification should follow. This procedure may vary considerably in different churches. In most cases, however, it involves at least three relationships: (1) to the church's ecclesiastical authority or regional executive; (2) to the local church council; (3) to the local church membership.

In some churches, such as the Episcopal Church, the procedure begins with a report to and approval by the diocesan bishop. In other churches, such as the United Church of Christ and Baptist Churches, where local autonomy is emphasized, the ecclesiastical executive may be consulted or informed, but often only after a congregational meeting has been called and a final vote upon the committee's recommendation has been taken. In some churches, the search committee may report to the church council, which, in turn, ratifies (or rejects) the recommendation. In still others, the council may seek approval from the entire membership in an announced, open meeting at which a vote is taken.

In those churches in which there is no required approval or consent by the ecclesiastical authority or regional executive, it is still a sound practice for the committee to consult with the executive officer before issuing a call. This step provides another check to disclose any hidden problems, and it also builds better relationships with the regional leadership.

As a general procedure, most search committees will consult informally with the candidate they have selected before proceeding to the reporting and ratification steps, in order to determine if the candidate will accept the call. Usually the chair handles this matter in an informal conversation. It is particularly important at this stage and hereafter to keep the candidate informed about each development and action in the calling process.

Informing the Candidates

Once the search committee has made its selection, communication with all of the candidates becomes a sensitive matter that also involves certain moral issues. Some committees choose not to inform the candidates of their decision until the selected candidate decides to accept or reject a call. In itself, there probably is nothing particularly unethical in such a procedure. There is a serious moral problem, however, when a candidate declines and a committee then proceeds to a second or third choice *without* disclosing this fact to the candidates. Such a practice is dishonest and conceals significant information from the candidates. Open and honest communication with all of the candidates concerning the committee's decision is the path to be followed. And it is courteous and honorable to inform quickly all of the candidates not selected.

Chapter Six

Negotiations

Sam Bass was selected by a unanimous and enthusiastic vote of the search committee of Mt. Zion Church to be its new senior pastor, and Sam indicated that he would accept the call. Prior to the committee's decision he had reviewed with the committee's chair and the chair of the church council the terms of employment, including the salary and benefits package to be provided. Sam was pleased with the job description and the salary offered, but the house provided for the minister needed considerable renovation; he and his wife wanted an unfinished third floor to be made into two bedrooms and a bathroom to house two of their five children. The council and committee heads assured Sam that there would be no problem in making these repairs and alterations. Another area of negotiation concerned time for continuing education and study. Sam made a case for three weeks of study time in addition to his one month vacation. Although the committee and council had not made provision for study time, the heads promised Sam that the council would go along with his request.

Five days prior to the announced congregational meeting to vote on the search committee's selection, the terms of Sam's call and employment were presented to the Mt. Zion Church's council for approval, and a major disagreement broke out. The church's treasurer and the head of the property committee were enraged at the proposed renovations on the house and demanded that these requests be substantially altered and reduced, including elimination of the third floor renovations. They argued that the previous conversations they had been involved in had included an agreement only for repainting the house and some minor alterations. Moreover, three other members of the council joined the treasurer in objecting adamantly to giving the new pastor any study time for continuing education. "We never did this before" was the heart of their shrill objection. The council's chair and other members of the search committee who served on the council were told by the angry opponents that they must renegotiate the terms with Sam before they would vote approval of his call. Bowing to this pressure, the council and search committee chairs called Sam the next day and asked him to drop his requests for the continuing education time and the planned renovation of the house's third floor. Regarding the latter, Sam was told that the treasurer was agreeable to having the church pay for the renovation as long as Sam reimbursed the church in full within one year. The two committee chairs apologized and sought to assure Sam: "Something can be worked out next year after you've been here awhile." Sam responded that he had been given assurances and promises guaranteeing these items, and upon that basis he had given them his agreement. Now, four days before the congregational meeting, there is an impasse.

* * *

Gordon Wainwright accepted the call to be pastor of Second Church, and as the senior deacon and senior trustee put it, "We agreed on things with a handshake all around." Inasmuch as Gordon had felt stuck in his previous parish and was eager to leave it, he did not press matters after he negotiated a higher salary and found that the house provided by Second Church was a considerable improvement over the one his family would be leaving. Moreover, the senior deacon and trustee seemed to be reasonable people with whom one could reach agreement. Several months later, however, Gordon had come to think that the agreement was the handshake that shook him down.

Moving costs were the first problem that Gordon encountered with Second Church. Although the search committee, the senior deacon and senior trustee had assured Gordon that the church would pay for moving his family, when the mover's statement arrived, the church's treasurer would pay only half of it, saying that the Wainwrights had "too much stuff" and that Second Church couldn't afford the entire amount. After a protracted hassle among Gordon, the treasurer, the trustee, and the deacon, a compromise was reached: Second Church paid three-fourths, and Gordon paid one-fourth of the bill.

At the end of Gordon's first month, a second "shake-down" took place. This time it concerned automobile expenses. Gordon had been told by the trustee to submit a mileage total each month for reimbursement. The treasurer demanded that Gordon submit odometer readings and that the church could only pay eight cents a mile. Gordon pointed out that the recommended IRS allowance was 20 cents per mile and that others pay even higher rates. Again, after numerous hours wasted in protracted negotiations, a compromise of twelve cents per mile was reached, and the demand for odometer readings was dropped.

At the second trustees' meeting following Gordon's arrival, a disagreement developed over the pastor's schedule. Three trustees wanted the minister in the office from 9:00 A.M. to 3:00 P.M. each day, whereas two other trustees wanted the pastor out calling on parishioners and new prospects every day rather than sitting around the office. At the meeting's 11:00 P.M. adjournment, nothing was settled, and Gordon was certain that the subject would come up again.

Finally, the property committee chair and the treasurer met with Gordon in the church office. They complained about the amounts of electricity and heating oil being used in the pastor's house. After an unpleasant conversation, they pointedly admonished Gordon to "turn the thermostat down" and use the lights and appliances less.

*　　*　　*

Conducting the Negotiations

The experience of Mt. Zion Church and Second Church illustrates some of the pitfalls commonly experienced by churches during the negotiations for calling a new pastor (Step 10). The problems are manifold: imprecise terms and conditions that are subject to different interpretations; unspecified conditions; lack of agreement among all those who will be involved with approving and implementing the terms; expectations that are too high and never fulfilled; expectations that are unrealistically low or restrictive and repressive.

The diffusion of power in democratically organized and congregationally operated churches is often the seat of perplexities, problems, and troubles when it comes to the terms and conditions of a pastor's call and employment. There is seldom a straight and clear line of authority and accountability in the operation and governing of churches. This often leads to multiple centers of power that inevitably come into disagreement and conflict. For the clergy, this means that they must become politicians attempting to balance and satisfy the various powers. Frequently the clergy are caught in the middle of various factions or viewpoints, and find themselves continually "on the spot." For churches, this means that sometimes the disparate viewpoints and struggles to dominate among various proponents make it unusually difficult to reach a harmonious, clear-cut, and unified set of terms and conditions of employment.

Within churches that use a committee system for calling a pastor there is a variety of organizations and procedures that affect the negotiations. Let's begin with the search committee. In talking with prospective pastors the committee needs to describe the basic terms and conditions that are offered with the post. Often these terms have been developed and determined by another group—a church council, a ruling session, a vestry, or a board of trustees. Whatever the nomenclature (for convenience we shall use "council"), the elected governing body of the local church usually makes the final decisions concerning finances, employment, use of the property, and basic policies and programs. In some cases the church's bylaws, constitution, or canons specify many procedures and practices that the council must follow. In other cases there are less formal structures. By comparison, the search committee is an unusual and rather ambiguous creature within the church: It is not permanent, and it has a specific mandate and job to do. It is dependent upon the decisions of other bodies to do its job and conduct its negotiations or conversations. Therefore, the committee must have a clear and complete understanding of the council's terms and decisions if it is to accomplish its job. This necessity points out the importance of having one or more members of the council (including the council chair) serve on the search committee.

In a recent case, the senior warden of the vestry (the chair of the governing body) of an Episcopal Church was not part of the search committee. In the process of making a selection and conducting negotiations, there was considerable game playing, conflict, and blocking between some of the committee members and some of the vestry. Once the committee had made its choice and recommendation, and the vestry was left to handle the negotiations, the senior warden used the negotiation process to question and reopen the selection itself. Generally speaking, although the search committee discusses terms and conditions of the call with candidates, it does not set those terms or handle the final negotiations. In one sense, its job draws to a close when it makes a selection, and another body takes over to conduct the negotiations and make an agreement.

When the church council has accepted the search committee's selection, its officers or designated representatives must negotiate an agreement with the newly selected pastor. If members of the council have been an integral part of the committee's work, this task will be a relatively simple one. Often it is merely the formality of putting into a final form what has already been discussed. In other cases, only a general outline or sketch of the terms and conditions may have been discussed previously, so detailed negotiations are needed to reach an agreement. In some churches, the council or governing board simply has to follow the procedures or rules of the church's codes or constitution for implementing decisions and agreements. But even in these circumstances, ambiguities or difficulties arise from time to time.

One of the most frequent problems in negotiating clergy employment concerns expenditures and payments: Will the treasurer adhere to the agreements and terms approved by the council? This is not a superfluous question, for more than one church treasurer has blocked, frustrated, and destroyed agreements to which the treasurer objected. Resolving this kind of deadlock requires strong, unified action on the part of the council. Such action, however, is often difficult to obtain. And even if the council can succeed, considerable damage and injury might have already been done. Far better is the situation in which the council and the financial officers are in harmony about the terms and conditions which are negotiated and agreed upon with the new pastor. Similarly, there also should be agreement in the council and among all those who will be involved in other areas of policy and practice, such as property use, office administration, education, worship, and music. The church's various power centers and officers must work in tandem under the leadership of the head of the governing body if the negotiations are to be conducted and concluded in a clear-cut and unequivocal manner. Anything less is deceptive and fraudulent.

Not only should all concerned be informed and their consent obtained so that there is no backing down or undoing of agreements (as in Gordon Wainwright's experience), but there needs to be a clear, fully detailed, and *unified* agreement on the terms and conditions of the call. Committee and governing bodies should ask themselves:

• Are there ambiguities in the negotiations, such as a double standard of job expectations and goals that may lead to confusion later on?
• Are there conditions and terms within the agreement that contradict each other?
• Is either party being asked to agree to the impossible?

The council must handle its negotiations with care and attention to avoid these kinds of problems. When an agreement finally has been concluded, the council should examine it again, asking the questions:

• Are these terms fair and reasonable?
• Are these terms workable?

What Should Be Covered?

There are two general parts to the terms and conditions of ministry that have to be covered in the negotiations: (1) the clergy's professional duties; (2) the clergy's compensation.

The experience of Gordon Wainwright demonstrates why it is necessary for pastors and churches to reach a clear and reasonably detailed agreement concerning the pastor's duties. Frequently, church committees and councils operate on the presupposition that "we all know what the pastor's job is." In fact, different people often hold vastly different, and even contradictory, notions about the pastor's job. A relatively effective way to approach this matter is to develop a job description, a two-part list of duties and responsibilities. The first part should list those duties that the pastor personally performs. The second part should list those duties for which the pastor supervises or trains others, including staff, volunteers, and church officers. When developing the job description, the committee needs to find a balance between the extremes of a list that is too detailed and hence confining and one that is too ambiguous and hence meaningless.

Clergy job descriptions prepared by lay committees or church councils and boards invariably portray one of three contrasting pictures or images. Some are looking for someone to manage a business corporation. Others seek a mechanic with a bag of tools and plans to come into the shop and get the machine rebuilt and operating smoothly. Still others seek a public affairs, good-will person who will make an impact on the community and attract large numbers of new dues-paying members. In each of these pictures there is little or no perception of the true nature of the church, its historic tradition, or its ministry. This lack of perception is not surprising; it is neither good or bad. Rather, it simply reflects that lay people should not be expected to have a theologically sophisticated perception of the ministry. Nor should they be expected to become educated and trained in that perception, for a search committee can function effectively without such sophistication. However, a search committee or church council of lay people *should be expected* to recognize both that developing a job description of clergy duties is an extraordinary matter and that they need professional help to do so. Thus, seeking the advice, counsel, and guidance of an outside clergy consultant—an interim or supply pastor, or a synod, presbytery, or diocesan officer—should be an integral part of the process of developing the clergy job description. Finally, the newly selected pastor should become the committee's counsel of last resort, for that is the person who is being called to be the pastor.

All too frequently the attitude of church councils and search committees is, "We know what we need and want; it's our church; we write the rules." This attitude can never be justified in the Christian tradition, and it reflects a woefully twisted notion of Christ's church. The church is not *our* church or anyone's church; it belongs to Jesus Christ and to him alone. The local church is but a part of the larger whole and therefore owes its allegiance to that higher community—the historic community of Christian faith and practice. The local church is not an autonomous club or lodge or fraternity or sorority of dues-paying members. So, too, the clergy are not hired hands placed at the beck and call of a dues-paying membership. Rather, the clergy are those members of the church who are trained and set apart by ordination to represent the whole of Christ's church by serving the local body. The local committee or council that presumes to write the pastor's job description without clergy advice and counsel is acting in a way similar to the lay committee or board of a hospital that presumes to direct a surgeon in handling the details of a complex surgical procedure. Therefore, writing this description requires a full and balanced perspective of what it takes to embody faithfully the church's ministry. That perspective is most adequately arrived at with the teaching, guidance, and assistance of those whom the church has trained and set apart for this calling.

In the next section of this chapter some sample agreements and forms are provided that can serve as checklists of details to be included in the second part of negotiations, namely the question of clergy compensation. Before looking at those samples, however, we need to note some general principles. In addition to salary, clergy compensation has traditionally included housing with utilities, medical and hospital insurance, retirement pensions, reimbursement for transportation needed to perform clergy duties, vacation time, provisions for professional study and education, and some provision for clergy vestments (where used). Specified allotments for clergy supplies (books, vestments, etc.) should be reviewed annually because of inflation in prices in our society. One person's high price is another's low price, and adequate monies should be available to perform the requisite duties.

Supplemental benefits and provisions are more than justified, since clergy salaries are much lower than those of similarly trained professionals in our society. Any comparison of clergy salaries with those of industry, government, or other professions quickly substantiates this claim. To be certain, those who seek ordination and a life of ministry are electing a life of service and denial, and they do not belong in the calling if financial earnings are their highest goal. Nevertheless, clergy should neither be forced to live without adequate provision nor be expected to underwrite the local church's budget.

Because clergy have an irregular work schedule that includes Sundays and being on call at all times for emergencies and crises, it is necessary that provision be made for other time off during the week. Whatever the formula used to determine the normal work week, it should include the reasonable expectation of five work days. The nature of clergy duties is such that the weekly schedule actually can be computed or calculated only by the pastor. Large segments of the clergy's time are devoted to confidential matters of pastoral care to which no one else is privy. Other unseen time—and it should be substantial—is devoted to study and preparation for worship, preaching, and teaching, and to prayer. A clergy contract should affirm this unique aspect of the pastor's duties, and with trust grant to the pastor a large measure of freedom to perform those duties. Basically, what a church does when it calls a pastor is to select someone with the personal and professional competence necessary to determine what the job is and then to do it.

Employment Contracts and Agreements

In recent years it has become a recommended procedure in many churches for a formal, written employment contract to be signed at the time of calling a new pastor. A variety of forms and types of contracts have been developed by clergy associations, synods, presbyteries, dioceses, and state conferences of churches. Most of these agreements are divided into the two parts that we have already discussed, professional duties and professional compensation. The extent of detail incorporated into the contracts varies considerably. Some agreements cover every possible function and benefit, while others provide a more general outline that emphasizes certain major items. To provide some practical assistance to committees and church councils, we are reproducing two sample agreements: The Massachusetts Episcopal Clergy Association Job Description and Letter of Call/Agreement and a General Letter of Agreement used by a variety of churches. The general form is an uncomplicated one that emphasizes the bonds being established between the parish and pastor and the commitment made to ministry. It is usually accompanied by a single page that itemizes the financial terms and commitments of employment. In contrast, the Massachusetts form is a detailed and lengthy one. Each form has certain strengths and weaknesses, so we encourage committees to study them with an eye to adapting and developing the material to fit their particular situations. Although any search committee or church council is well advised to have developed at least an outline prior to negotiating with a new pastor, the final form and details of the agreement have to be a joint endeavor of the two parties. It is unrealistic and insulting for any church to hand the new pastor a prepared agreement on a take-it-or-leave-it basis.

* * *

A FORM FOR JOB DESCRIPTION AND LETTER OF AGREEMENT
between Rectors and Congregations of the Episcopal Church, adaptable for Vicars, part-time and non-stipendiary clergy

Developed by the Massachusetts Episcopal Clergy Association[1]

JOB DESCRIPTION
to be updated annually

OUTLINE

1. Title of the position.

2. A brief summary of the purpose of the parish in its given situation.

3. The basic function of the position and its relationship to the purpose.

4. Specific areas of duty and responsibility (shared and separate) to be undertaken by Rector and Vestry/Congregation, including:
   A. Leadership of worship
   B. Administration of sacraments
   C. Preaching
   D. Teaching of adults
   E. Teaching of children
   F. Working with/teaching youth
   G. Visiting in homes

H. Visiting in times of crisis or sickness
I. Counselling
J. Administration of the parish
K. Administration of buildings/property
L. Stewardship and fund-raising
M. Evangelism/membership
N. Participation in community projects and issues
O. Inter-church cooperation
P. Enabling social ministries of the congregation
Q. Theological learning and reflection
R. Participation in the Diocese and National Church
S. Organizing groups and committees

5. Mutual Accountability: What are the expectations, responsibilities, and relationships between the following: Clergyperson; Vestry; Employed Staff; Volunteers; Committees; Diocese. (Refer to goals, parish bylaws, diocesan and national canons, etc.)

6. Specific long-term goals and short-term goals for development of the parish or the leadership skills of the clergyperson and laity (results expected within a year).

7. Some standard of performance-evaluation of all parties— satisfactory to all parties—will be utilized annually at a time separate from (and prior to) the setting of compensation.

8. The date for the next updating of this Job Description.

LETTER OF CALL/AGREEMENT
between

The Reverend _____

The Vestry of _____
Parish (or Congregation)

which has elected him/her to be Rector, with the understanding that his/her Rectorship shall continue until dissolved by mutual consent or by arbitration and decision as provided by Title III, Canon 21, of the General Convention.

The terms of this Letter of Agreement shall be reviewed and updated annually.

SECTION A. TIME OF WORK

The Vestry expects the Rector of this Parish to work _____ days per week, take _____ days off per week, and work no more than _____ hours per week. It is understood that he/she will be on call at other times in case of emergency.

SECTION B. COMPENSATION

1. The rector's annual cash stipend will be $_____, from which the Rector will pay his/her own Social Security.

2. Housing will be provided to the Rector according to the following arrangement (strike out the one which does not apply):

   a. Annual Housing Allowance (including utilities), to be used in accord with Reg. 1.107 of the I.R.S., in the amount of $_____.

   b. The use of the Rectory. The Vestry assumes responsibility for the following expenses of maintaining the house:
   —Utilities costs as charged (except personal long distance telephone tolls).
   —Expenses for repair, remodeling, and appliances as follows:_____
   _____.

   —The Rector agrees to the following responsibilities for maintenance of the house and grounds:_____
   _____.

3. The Vestry agrees to pay the following premiums:

   a. Church Pension Fund premiums on the Rector's stipend.

b. Life Insurance premiums on the Rector as required by the Diocese.

c. Health and Accident Insurance premiums, consistent with Diocesan guidelines.

d. Disability Insurance premiums as follows:_____
_____.

4. In the event of the total disability of the Rector, the following agreements apply:
   a. Regarding housing:_____.
   b. Regarding compensation:_____.

5. In case of the death of the Rector, the following agreements apply:
   a. Regarding housing of the family:_____.
   b. Regarding compensation to the family:_____
   _____.

SECTION C. EXPENSES

The Vestry agrees to pay for the following expenses incurred by the Rector in fulfilling his/her professional duties:

1. Travel: The Rector is granted a travel (automobile) allowance of $_____ annually

   OR

   is to be reimbursed at the rate of _____ cents per mile

   OR

   is to be provided with an automobile, with allowance for its maintenance and operation.
   (Strike out provisions which do not apply.)

2. Communications: The Vestry agrees to provide for a telephone in the Rector's office and study. All postage for church business will be included in the parish budget.

3. Office: All necessary office furniture, equipment, and supplies will be paid for by the parish, the amount to be established in the annual budget.

4. Moving: In the case of an initial Letter of Call, the Vestry will defray the cost of packing and moving the Rector's household goods in full, up to the amount of $_____.

5. Discretionary Fund: A fund of $_____ per year will be provided for charities and expenditures at the discretion of the Rector. Additional funding and special arrangements for this are as follows:_____.

6. Guests and Hospitality: The amount of $_____ will be included in the parish budget for the obtaining of guest preachers, speakers, musicians, etc. (in addition to vacation supply). The Rector will be given an allowance (or reimbursed) for the cost of hospitality and entertainment on behalf of the parish up to the amount of $_____.

7. Dues of the Rector to the Massachusetts Episcopal Clergy Association and other professional associations, and the cost of professional periodicals, will be paid by the parish up to the amount of $_____.

8. Continuing Education
   a. The Rector may spend up to $_____ annually (with the option to accumulate unspent portions up to seven years) to further his/her professional education.
   b. Pulpit supply and pastoral services shall be funded by the parish during periods of absence for continuing education, as detailed below.

SECTION D. LEAVE TIME

The Vestry agrees that the Rector shall have the following periods of leave at full pay:

1. Days off as indicated in Section A. These days will normally be: _____.

2. _____ weeks of vacation per year, including _____ Sundays (at least one month).

3. _____ weeks per year (in addition to vacation time) for continuing education and career development (at least two weeks).

4. _____ days of sick leave per year, cumulative to a maximum of _____ days (additional sick leave to be considered in relation to Disability Insurance).

5. Six months paid time off for Sabbatical Leave (continuing education, research, and reflection) for every seven years in the ministry, the first to occur in the year _____. (Funding for such leave should be anticipated annually in the budget and include Sabbatical expenses and clergy supply expenses.)

SECTION E. SUPPLEMENTARY COMPENSATION

The following understanding has been reached between the Rector and the Vestry concerning the income the Rector may receive performing the rites of the church or from teaching, counselling, lecturing, writing, and providing consultative services:

_____.

SECTION F. USE OF BUILDINGS

In addition to his/her use and control of Parish buildings for the discharge of his/her duties, the Rector shall have the right to grant use of the buildings to individuals or groups from outside the Parish under the following conditions:

_____.

The Vestry shall make the decision for use of the church and buildings by outside individuals or groups under the following circumstance:

_____.

SECTION G. EVALUATION AND REVISION

This agreement is to be revised annually at the time that the Rector's work is evaluated and before compensation is set for the following year. The Rector and Vestry agree to an annual discussion and evaluation of one another's work in the Parish, the purpose being:

1. To provide the clergyperson with a more accurate picture of how the congregation sees him/her than might be received informally.

2. To allow the clergyperson to evaluate how the Vestry is fulfilling its responsibilities to him/her.

3. To establish goals (in addition to Parish goals) for the work of Rector and Vestry in the coming year.

4. To isolate areas of conflict or disappointment which have not received adequate attention and may be adversely affecting working relationships.

5. To clarify expectations on both sides, which will help put future conflicts in a manageable form.

6. To provide an additional and valuable factor for the Vestry to use in setting future compensation.

The date of the first such evaluation following this agreement is: _____.

SECTION H. OTHER AGREEMENTS

SECTION I. DISAGREEMENT OR RESERVATION

The Rector and Vestry make note of specific areas of disagreement between them as follows:_____
_____.

SECTION J. SIGNATURES

Date: _____   *Rector:* _____
Date: _____   *Warden:* _____

*   *   *

GENERAL LETTER OF AGREEMENT

Between

_____

(church)

and

_____

(pastor)

The Pastor and Church Council agree that the relationship between Pastor and parish shall be one of a joint endeavor in which by God's grace they are joined together in obedience to the Gospel of Jesus Christ.

It shall be the Pastor's ministry to lead the church through the exercise of (his/her) ordained ministry in blessing and bestowing forgiveness in God's name, in faithfully observing the sacraments, in teaching and preaching the Word of God for the salvation of the world and the guidance of God's people; by administering the work of this church to God's glory; and by offering of self as pastor and friend to all those whose lives the ministry of this church touches.

The Church Council accepts its responsibility to provide to the best of the capacity of the church the tools and resources required for this ministry, and to lead the people of this church by an example of prayer, worship, giving and faithfulness, and to encourage people to exercise their ministries as God calls them to do so. In this they will support and strengthen the ministry of the Pastor by their prayers, their friendship and good will, their counsel, their time, their ability and their generosity.

/s/   /s/

_____   _____

Pastor   For the Church Council

What More Is Needed?

In conducting negotiations, every church body needs to ask itself, "What more is needed in these matters? Has the committee or council been fair and equitable in its terms and offer? Is a commensurate measure of goodwill and trust evident?" These negotiations should not be an adversary proceeding. The relationship between pastor and parish is not an ordinary employer-employee relationship and should not be considered or spoken about in those terms. More than anything else, enthusiasm and respect for the pastor will help insure a satisfactory conclusion of negotiations and a positive beginning for this new ministry.

Finally, the pastoral relationship requires a measure of flexibility in expectations and how they are fulfilled. No church can find everything it wants or needs in one pastor, and no pastor can find the perfect church. Nevertheless, once it has been decided to call a pastor because that particular person fits best, then reasonable adjustments of expectations need to be made on all sides. Obviously there are certain abilities and skills that are necessary for ministry but beyond these there are many skills and duties in which different people have different degrees of talent. In these the pastor's strengths and skills should be allowed to flourish without being upset and overturned by other deficiencies or shortcomings. If the committee has done its job thoroughly, it will have been aware of the pluses and minuses and decided to proceed because this pastor was the best one for the church. Now it is incumbent upon everyone to live with that decision and help realize its fullest potential.

Footnote

1. Used by permission of the Massachusetts Episcopal Clergy Association.

Chapter Seven

It Doesn't End
with the Call

The search committee has made its selection, the church's official board has approved and concluded its negotiations with the new pastor, and the members have ratified the decision by vote in a special church meeting. Has the work ended? For the search committee the answer is yes, for it ceases to exist when the call is issued and accepted. In a larger sense, however, this is not simply the end but also a new beginning for everyone in the church and perhaps especially for those who have been part of the search committee. The interest and support developed within the committee during its brief life need to be dispersed and kept alive throughout the congregation. The committee's interest and support need to be translated into an ongoing and deepening support of the new ministry. This is not to say that a new ministry stands or falls on the basis of a single committee's support. But multiple centers of renewal and points of growth can spring up and develop in the aftermath of the calling process. Under the best of circumstances, as the committee is discharged, its members will recognize that its mission doesn't end with the call: Each member carries out into the church and the future a special interest and responsibility for the health of the church's ministry. Surely any committee will have learned much during its search. I hope that such learning will have led to a sounder theological appreciation of the church and its ministry—an appreciation that manifests itself in increased support and dedication to that ministry.

Most new pastors need and welcome that kind of interest and support.

In some churches it is now a practice to convert the search committee into a council of advice and support for the first year of the new pastorate. There is both positive and negative potential in this practice, and each parish and its new pastor will need to determine if this is something that they want to have for the first year. One could argue that this is a superfluous step, as well as a potentially divisive one, because the church's governing board holds the official responsibility for advising and supporting the ministry. Nevertheless, some church governing boards have recommended and encouraged this step with positive results. The search group will have a certain cohesiveness and esprit de corps if it has functioned with purpose and harmony. That kind of interest and energy can become a regular source of support and counsel for the new pastor, while also being a center of interpretation and support flowing out to the congregation.

If the search committee has experienced major difficulty in completing its job or if the process has been a particularly divisive one, then the committee should die quickly and not be converted to a council of advice. There is nothing to be proved or gained in perpetuating bad conditions. As a general principle, any such conversion should not continue beyond a year's time, in order to insure that the group does not begin to regard itself as a permanent body.

What we have said about the parish applies with equal weight to the permanent boards, committees, and councils of the entire church once it has called a minister. The ongoing life of the church and its pastor needs the continuing interest and support of the people. To be certain, clergy are the full-time leaders, centers of inspiration and guidance, and the religious teachers of the community. But they cannot do everything alone. Once the call has been completed, it is tempting for church's members to retire and let the pastor do it. But if anything has been realized in a larger sense during the calling process, it ought to be the significance and importance of an ongoing interest, involvement, and support for the church. The search committee's call of a new pastor is both the end of its task and the beginning of a new and larger task for the entire parish, namely, its future ministry and witness in the world.

Appendix

The Assistant Pastor

From time to time many churches also use a committee to call assistant or associate pastors. Because the assistant pastor's post is substantially different from that of the pastor, the search and calling process entails some needs and considerations that are somewhat different from those we have discussed in this book. This appendix is added to guide committees, church councils, and clergy to meet those special needs and considerations.

The Assistant Pastor's Post

The assistant pastor's position is not as much a post as it is a perilous perch, according to many who have occupied it during their careers. At best, the post is an anomaly for most clergy, because it is so different from what they have been prepared and trained to expect and accomplish. The assistant's role is a specialized one, in which the range of clergy duties and responsibilities is usually restricted and confined to one or more designated areas. It is also an entirely dependent post, in which the assistant is under the supervision and tenure of the pastor. Finally, it is a post in which some of the fundamental duties and skills of ministry are rarely practiced.

Generally speaking, four kinds of clergy are likely to be called to assistantships: those just out of seminary, those heading toward retirement or in semiretirement; those who have made a decision to occupy such a post rather than be the pastor of a parish; and those who have not been able to secure a call to be a pastor. It is with the first of these groups that some of the most troubling problems are to be found.

Although the assistantship has often been seen as an apprenticeship, its benefits for those just coming out of seminary should be examined critically. Many assistantships postpone necessary learning and set up unnecessary handicaps for newly ordained and inexperienced clergy. An assistantship is often a limited ministry in which several vital functions—such as preaching, officiating at baptisms, marriages and funerals, leading the church council, teaching adults—are performed infrequently. Moreover, the assistant generally receives little practice in essentials that are going to be called for on a regular basis when one is the pastor of a parish. Furthermore, the assistant's ministry is often concentrated on one or two groups of people within the parish. This tends to provide a very limited and restricted experience that, in turn, may hinder the person's spiritual development and growth. Because many parishes that require assistant pastors are sufficiently large enough to involve an organization and structure that is never found in the average parish, care must be taken to provide a balanced perspective of ministry.

Exposure to this kind of large operation may create some unusual dependencies for the assistant, in part because many senior clergy are poor apprentice masters who neither train others well nor delegate and share duties with ease or skill. Before the search committee decides what kind of assistant pastor it is seeking, it should ask:

• Does your pastor share duties and responsibilities easily and skillfully?

• Is your pastor capable and willing to train and supervise other clergy?

In answering these questions, the committee needs to be unusually honest and forthright without feeling that it is challenging its pastor. Some senior clergy simply are not capable of handling these matters in a positive and affirmative way, yet often they are not aware of that incapability. This deficiency should not be judged negatively; but it should be recognized, in order to avoid calling the kind of assistant who needs those very things that cannot be given by this particular pastor.

Some senior clergy are wise and capable apprentice masters, but we suspect that they are in the minority. Therefore no parish should be too surprised to recognize that its pastor is not one of these. In such cases, rather than calling a newly ordained person, the parish and its pastor may be best served by calling another experienced pastor who has chosen, for one reason or another, to serve as an assistant.

Even when an assistant pastor comes with previous parish experience, the assistantship can be a difficult and vexing post because of its restricted nature and the role of the pastor. If you decide to call an experienced pastor who has chosen for one reason or another to be an assistant, you need to discover those reasons, evaluate them, and decide if they can be the basis for a sound working relationship. The most reliable basis for an assistantship is the forthright recognition—so stated by everyone involved—that the post is a dependent and limited one. For many clergy, an assistantship is a way station along the road to becoming a pastor. Any committee or pastor that thinks the assistantship is a co-equal ministry, is deluding itself and laying the groundwork for a disappointing failure.

Having acknowledged these limitations, we should recognize that there are sound reasons for some clergy to become assistant pastors and remain in those posts on a long-term basis. These include clergy who recognize special strengths in certain areas and deficiencies in others, clergy who feel called to this specialized ministry, clergy whose training and background have been concentrated in a given area, and those who are comfortable with the subordinate role.

Before concluding this topic, we need to turn to the other side of the coin, so to speak, and recognize that assistant pastors often pose major problems for pastors. Although youthful exuberance and inexperience may be near the top of the list of problems created by assistants, probably the most serious ones are those caused by disloyalty. Whether because of a growing dissatisfaction with the limited role of assistant or because of outright theological or administrative disagreements, it is not uncommon for assistants to foster dissention in the parish and begin to undercut the pastor's position. In those cases where assistant pastors are working primarily with one group within the parish and have enjoyed success and popularity, an acute myopia can develop. As a consequence, the assistant may begin to believe that a particular, but limited, success points to an invincible ability that is often being thwarted by the pastor. In this myopic world, it is but a short step from believing in one's invincibility to believing that one should be the pastor. Whatever the circumstances of dissatisfaction may be, these situations can result in serious damage to everyone—the pastor, the assistant, and the parish. Resolving such problems is another subject. Our attention is focused on the search committee and the selection process. The most critical task of such committees is to be fully aware of the liabilities of the assistantship and then to exert every effort and skill to select a person who is capable of filling the post in harmony with the pastor.

The Search Process

Because the assistant pastor's post has handicaps and limitations, special attention and consideration is required in the search process. The process is also quite different than that of other searches because it will involve the pastor as the principal member and leader. In most churches that use committees to select assistant pastors, the committee will have been appointed with the advice and consent of the pastor, who should be the leader and principal voice in the committee, even if it is chaired by another person. Because the crucial relationship for any assistantship is with the pastor, the search committee will need to place its top priority on this relationship in order to make the best selection.

Although it makes no sense for a search committee to choose an assistant who is not acceptable to the pastor, there are situations in which a committee may need to advise and even convince a pastor about the kind of assistant that is appropriate for the parish. As mentioned earlier, there are senior clergy who lack the necessary abilities or the will to function with an assistant. In such a situation, the search committee, like the church's council, needs to face and resolve the problem with its pastor. In some cases, it is best solved by helping the pastor to realize his or her limitations and then seeking the kind of assistant who fits into the situation with all of its limitations and liabilities. In other cases, the only acceptable course to follow is to employ unordained lay workers to assist the pastor.

There are senior clergy who have histories of consistently undermining or destroying assistants and who are incapable of working with them in a decent and humane way. This kind of pastor is better off working with a staff of lay people. In some cases, this is far better than the twisted and tortured path of multiple-clergy staffs, where the senior pastor is an intolerable autocrat or an incompetent manager and leader. In such situations, the church council or even a search committee has a special responsibility and opportunity to help its pastor face reality and deal with it in a forthright and positive manner. Similarly the council or the search committee needs to counsel its pastor against selecting a potentially disruptive or uncooperative assistant. Sometimes a committee is able to identify such persons more clearly than the pastor and to act to save the pastor and parish from an unfortunate situation.

For the parish whose pastor works well with assistants, the search committee should rely on the pastor to lead the search process. The committee's primary role, then, is to be a source of advice and support to its pastor in seeking an assistant. Its other function is to give prospective assistants a cross-sectional view of and introduction to the congregation. We believe that pastors should do their own initial searches and screening, rather than delegate this job. No pastor is too busy to gather a sufficient number of names and recommendations of suitable candidates with a few telephone calls. The pastor who is not willing to do so is likely to be the pastor who will handle an assistantship in a second-hand manner, and prospects for a successful pastor-assistant relationship are slim.

Although some clergy prefer to have the committee interview two or three acceptable candidates, in most cases the committee need meet and interview only the candidate selected by the pastor. Circumstances in which a committee dictates a choice or blocks the pastor's choice should be avoided. It makes no sense for a committee to force an assistant upon its pastor, nor does it make sense to block the pastor's choice unless there are clearly perceived and compelling obstacles that are agreed upon by the committee. In such relatively rare situations, the committee will need to vote its conscience and provide its best counsel to the pastor.

For the most part, the calling process for assistant pastors can be a relatively swift and clear one, guided and led by the pastor. The practice of some churches is not to involve a search committee at all, but simply to have the pastor appoint assistants with the consent of the governing body. Generally, this procedure makes sense, and I cannot see any particular need for a search committee unless the pastor asks for the advice and support that such a group can provide. Even if a parish does not use a search committee when seeking an assistant pastor, much of what has been said regarding the committee's role and the stages of the search process applies equally to situations in which the pastor handles the search and appointment alone.

When the Pastor Leaves

Assistant pastors are placed in an especially precarious situation when the pastor retires, dies, or departs for another parish. Some churches have specific procedures to handle these situations, such as requiring the resignation of assistants, but in others there is no prescribed procedure. Inevitably the parish must settle the question of whether the assistant should be called as its next pastor. In some cases the assistant will not be interested in the post, and so the matter is easily resolved. In most cases, however, the matter is more complicated. If the assistant has been in the parish for some time, there are likely to be strong pro and con sentiments about calling that person as the new pastor.

Although there is no right or clear solution to cover all cases of this kind, we are opposed to the rule that an assistant should never be called as the pastor in the same parish. Such rule is too inflexible, unnecessarily inequitable, and clearly discriminatory. There are numerous instances in which calling the assistant as the pastor has proven to be a very sound and productive choice. In one of the more extreme examples, a large parish passed over the senior assistant, who was a person of seasoned experience with demonstrated capabilities and an outstanding record of service to the church. He chose to stay when the church called a younger man as pastor (a far-shores syndrome choice) and handled the intervening years with unusual skill and patience. Within four years, however, and after a less than adequate performance, the new pastor was off for an even larger parish. This time the parish had the good sense to call as pastor the formerly passed-over assistant, and in the years since he has proven to be one of the best pastors in the parish's history.

In another example, a parish called its assistant minister as pastor, although he suffered from a crippling but not fatal chronic disease. There was considerable sentiment against his being called, and the vote was quite close. Now, over twelve years later, he has established a superior ministry in that community, and his special skills in working with the handicapped have become a new focus for that church. Of course, other examples could be cited where calling the assistant as the pastor has been a mistake. What I am suggesting in these situations is that the nature and capabilities of the person being called have proven to be far more important than whether or not the person has previously served as the parish's assistant.

When a pastor leaves and when the assistant pastor wishes to be considered for the post, the assistant should be given full review and consideration by the search committee. Of course, following this recommendation may present difficulties if the committee decides *not* to call the assistant. Sometimes when an assistant is not chosen as the new pastor, that person may want to move on to another parish as quickly as possible. Relations between the assistant and the person who is called to be the new pastor may prove difficult if the assistant feels rejected or stuck in the parish. Seldom does this develop into a healthy, pleasant, and productive relationship. More often than not, such assistants feel trapped in an excessively lengthy waiting period until they can find another position. It seems more practical and useful for the parish to offer assistant clergy a paid terminal year's leave of absence in such situations. This allows the new pastor an unemcumbered beginning, and it also provides the assistant with the necessary support and time to relocate. Such offers also permit departing clergy to take on interim ministries, in which cases an equitable division of payments could be arranged between the parishes involved. We urge parishes to prevent circumstances in which an assistant is passed over and then nothing substantial is done to help the person adjust or move.

Just as a newly called pastor assumes responsibility for the pastoral care of the parish, so too, whenever a church calls a pastor—be it the senior pastor or an assistant—it takes on certain responsibilities and obligations to that person. The church's responsibilities and obligations to its clergy should be measured and handled in terms of the highest standards and not simply in terms of those of the marketplace. Church councils and committees ought to conduct the church's business in a manner that is above reproach and sets an example.

Further Reading

About Pastors

The Christian Pastor by Wayne E. Oates, Philadelphia: Westminster Press, 1963.

Presents a comprehensive view of the ordained ministry and demonstrates the meaning and importance of pastors for the church and the world.

Minister on the Spot by James E. Dittes, Philadelphia: Pilgrim Press, 1970.

This intriguing view of all aspects of the pastoral vocation offers an unusual understanding of the conflicts, resistance, and frustrations experienced by pastors and also presents a unique description of the kinds of people that become clergy.

Too Many Pastors? by Jackson W. Carroll and Robert L. Wilson, New York: Pilgrim Press, 1980.

A survey and report of research about clergy employment and supply in the U.S.

Women As Pastors, ed. Lyle E. Schaller, Nashville: Abingdon Press, 1982.

Eleven women write about the various aspects of women as clergy.

Women of the Cloth by Jackson W. Carroll, Barbara Hargrove and Adair T. Lummis, San Francisco: Harper & Row, 1983.

A survey and research study of women clergy in the U.S.

About Churches

Decision Making in the Church: A Biblical Model by Luke T. Johnson, Philadelphia: Fortress Press, 1983.

An original study of the ways of decision making in the New Testament churches and communities.

The Fragmented Layman by Thomas C. Campbell & Yoshio Fukuyama, Philadelphia: Pilgrim Press, 1970.

Probably the most extensive and comprehensive survey and research yet conducted on the attitudes, beliefs, and religious practices of laity in the U.S. The authors found that lay people show fragmentation in their religious beliefs and practices and often hold contradictory opinions.

Small Churches Are Beautiful, ed. Jackson W. Carroll, New York: Harper & Row, 1977.

A reader on the function and place of small churches in contemporary American society.

The Unchurched by J. Russell Hale, New York: Harper & Row, 1980.

A narrative report of surveys and field studies of the attitudes and values of unchurched people in the U.S. The most complete and useful available study of the subject.

Understanding Church Growth, ed., Dean R. Hoge and David A. Roozen, New York: Pilgrim Press, 1979.

A collection of articles that gives a comprehensive view of church growth dynamics in the U.S.

The Well Church Book by Browne Barr, New York: Seabury Press, 1976.

How local churches can establish their well-being and remain faithful to the Gospel in today's world.

Where Have All the People Gone? New Choices for Old Churches by Carl S. Dudley, New York: Pilgrim Press, 1979.

Important ideas, information, and new strategies for older local churches.

253
M129

72771

About Ministry

A Biblical Basis for Ministry, ed. Earl E. Shelp & Ronald Sunderland, Philadelphia: Westminster Press, 1981.

Essays written by a number of biblical scholars on the scriptural foundations of ministry.

The Christian Ministry by J. B. Lightfoot, ed. with an introduction by Philip Edgcumbe Hughes, Wilton, Connecticut: Morehouse-Barlow, 1983.

The most significant and indispensible biblical study of the nature of ministry, written by a renowned English scholar and bishop.

The Gift of Administration by Thomas C. Campbell, Philadelphia: Westminster Press, 1981.

An important and original theological interpretation of administration in the church.

The Management of Ministry by James D. Anderson and Ezra Jones, New York: Harper & Row, 1978.

A comprehensive handbook of procedures and practices written from a managerial perspective.

The Ministering Congregation by Browne Barr and Mary Eakin, Philadelphia: Pilgrim Press, 1972.

How a congregation can become a ministering community that embodies Christian ideals in contemporary society.

The Purpose of the Church and Its Ministry by H. Richard Niebuhr, New York: Harper & Row, 1956.

For more than twenty-five years widely studied and considered indispensible for understanding and thinking about ministry.

When The People Say No by James E. Dittes, New York: Harper & Row, 1979.

An original and provocative interpretation of ministry that uncovers ways of understanding and dealing with resistance and obstruction.